GOD
SPOKE
TO ME

GOD SPOKE TO ME

Eileen Caddy

FINDHORN

© Eileen Caddy 1971
First published 1971
Reprinted six times
Second edition 1981
Second impression 1985
Third impression 1988

ISBN 0 905249 53 4

Set in 10/12 point Press Roman by Findhorn Publications
Printed and bound by Bookmag, Inverness
Published by The Findhorn Press,
Findhorn, Moray, Scotland

Cover design by Neil Baird

FOREWORD

It was in 1969 that a copy of *God Spoke to Me, Part 1,* first fell into my hands. At the time I had just undergone a seemingly calamitous sequence of events which, in a matter of weeks, had stripped me of my job, my flat, all of my personal belongings and savings, and my sense of purpose. Yet, throughout all this, I sensed the hand of God at work, leading me into something far better and more meaningful than I had known before. The friend who handed me the little booklet said, "Perhaps this is what you're looking for," and something told me that this was so. I opened the booklet at random, and my eyes fell upon the following words:

"Accept this day as a Special Day, a day of rebirth. This is My gift to you. You are being reborn in Spirit and in Truth. This is the biggest turning point in your life—from this day on, all is New.

"I want you to become aware of this and accept it as a fact now. You are to witness tremendous changes in your life and living. They may be gradual, but they will gather in momentum, and nothing will stop these changes, this transformation, from taking place. You will grow in stature; the old will pass away and *all* will be made new.

"You are now moving into the most glorious epoch of your life, for you know now the Truth. You know that I AM Life, that I AM Love, that I AM your consciousness and that I AM within you.

"This is something no one can take from you, that nothing can change. This is Reality. This is something which you have been seeking and now have found. It is the greatest treasure, the greatest Truth, for it brings you to that conscious Oneness with Me. Then you *know* that all I AM is thine and all I have is thine, and you are Mine.

"Let these truths become a part of you; absorb them as you breathe.

"They are the Breath of Life."

I knew that what I had read was true. The words may have come to me from without, but Something deep within me resonated to them in recognition and acceptance. The following day I left for Findhorn, and have been here ever since. That day, over three years ago, *was* undoubtedly the biggest turning point in my life. Tremendous changes *have* taken place since then and all *has* been made new. No longer need I seek without for the voice of God, for Findhorn has taught me to find that voice within.

Mine is only one of many stories which affirm the Truth and Wisdom contained within these pages. Over the years countless letters have been received from people whose lives have been radically changed and uplifted through reading *God Spoke to Me*, and many are those who have been drawn to Findhorn as a result of their own inner recognition of these Truths.

It is with a deep sense of gratitude and fulfilment that we present this newly revised and edited edition of *God Spoke to Me*, containing all four parts. May it serve to evoke that Source of Divinity from within you, as it has for countless others, that its Truths may become a part of you. Absorb them as you breathe—for they *are* the Breath of Life.

Roy McVicar

INTRODUCTION

It is in that inner peace and stillness that things begin to happen, and it was in that peace and stillness that I began to hear God's voice. This book, *God Spoke to Me*, contains some of the many messages which I have been given in this way over the last ten years. They have been edited, so that anything of a personal nature has been deleted.

All can hear that still small voice within. Try it. Be still and know that the I AM within you is God, the Beloved. Listen—then live by it. It really does work.

Eileen Caddy

CONTENTS

───────────── **PART 1 . . . . . page 13** ─────────────

79. Raise your thinking.
80. "Now are ye the sons of God."
81. Sound your own note.
82. Eliminate all "Ifs."
83. Self discipline.
84. Life glows and scintillates.
85. Live, live, live.

PEACE

86. See yourself as a chrysalis.
87. Great changes are about to take place.
88. Judge no man.
89. A Cloak of purest Light.

PRAISE

90. With praise on your lips.
91. A Song of Praise.

SEEK

92. The answers within.
93. There are many facets to a diamond.

94. Live by the Spirit.
95. Acceptance.
96. Skate confidently.
97. Life is full of surprises.
98. To become strong.
99. Seek first My kingdom and My Righteousness.

SPIRIT

100. Gifts of the Spirit.
101. Blessed is he who liveth by the Spirit.
102. You never know.
103. Life is what you make it.
104. Spirit is free.

TRUTH

105. This is My gift to you.
106. All I have is yours.
107. In Stillness find Truth.

———————— PART 2 . . . . . page 51 ————————

1. Three Commandments for the New Age.
2. Bring down My Heaven.
3. Peace.
4. Be Fearless.
5. This Instant of Time.
6. Living in the New.
7. Freedom of the Spirit.
8. Live Fully in the Moment.
9. Rise to Great Heights.
10. Make Time.
11. The Key.
12. Resistance Causes Suffering.
13. I Am with You.
14. A Time of Revelation.
15. Learn to Be.
16. Understanding.
17. Divine Economy.
18. Positive Thinking.
19. Lay All in My Hands.
20. Realisation.
21. My Love Is Limitless.
22. Know My Joy.
23. My Will Is Being Done.

24. Hold This Ideal.
25. Walk in My Ways.
26. I Am the Artist.
27. Do All with Me.
28. Sit and Be.
29. Bring Me into Everything.
30. All Are My Perfect Creation.
31. Live Reality.
32. Your Rock-like Foundation.
33. Be Conscious of Me.
34. The Individual Contribution.
35. There is the Perfect Answer.
36. The One Voice.
37. Greater Works Shall Ye Do.
38. Work by the Spirit.
39. Become as a Rock.
40. The Chrysalis.
41. Accept the Fact:
42. Behold My Wonders Coming About.
43. Life Is Like a Treasure Hunt.
44. When there is Conflict.
45. A Helping Hand.
46. Live My Word.
47. Grow in Stature.

—————— PART 3 . . . . . page 89 ——————

—————— PART 4 . . . . . page 103 ——————

GOD SPOKE TO ME

Part One

BE

ACCEPT PERIODS OF REST

1.   Just "being" is as essential as "doing". Enjoy life in its different phases, in its changing colours and moods. Watch the perfect pattern unfold and develop.

It is not what you say that matters. It is what you are and how you live.

Accept these periods of rest. I will make it clear when it is necessary for you to go into action.

PERFECT RHYTHM

2.   There are times of activity and there are times of peace. Learn to enjoy each state as it comes and realise how necessary this is.

There is the time for the indrawing of the breath of life and there is the time for expelling it.

There is perfect rhythm in all that is happening. Find peace and harmony within it.

MY WAYS

3.   My ways are strange and wonderful, but they are not man's ways. Therefore you find them baffling and bewildering. Learn to go with them, accept them.

How easy all this sounds in theory, but putting it into practice, living it every moment of the day and night is a different matter—yet words without action are empty and futile. Each must learn to live a life, hiding nothing. Strain comes when you cannot be your true Self and you are trying to hide something.

Learn to put people before things and be relaxed in all you do.

AWAITING THE OPPORTUNITY

4.   Wait on Me in absolute peace and confidence and know that I will reveal the Truth and that the Truth will set you free.

Those times when you can just Be are beneficial not only to you but to all you contact. Try more often to Be.

Times when you are alone are so precious; they are quite magical, as so much can happen in you and through you. I can so fill you that you become fully

God-conscious, a powerhouse for Love and Light to be generated and radiated out into the world. Wonders are awaiting to be revealed *through channels.*

CHOOSE MY WAY

5.   Be still and feel within you the rhythm of life and go with it. Make up your mind whether you wish to conform to man-made laws or to do My will whatever the costs. The choice lies in your own hands. You are free to choose and no one else can make the choice for you. Often the world will condemn you when you choose My way, but with My blessings you can face what is to come without flinching, and know that when you do My will only the perfect can be the final result.

RELAX!

6.   Relax! Give yourself over completely to Me.
There is much to be done but it can be done better in a less desperate hurry. Enjoy everything you do. Savour every action like a connoisseur. Be satisfied only with perfection.

"ALLOW MY CLOAK ..."

7.   Allow My cloak of peace and stillness to fall around you and envelop you completely. In quietness and confidence shall be your strength. I can work through you when you are in this state of consciousness no matter what you are doing.

ONE GLORIOUS WHOLE

8.   Be at peace. It is the opening of the heart centre which makes you feel everything so deeply. You find that tears flow so easily? These are tears of joy; let them flow. They are tears of recognition of Truth and Love divine. This brings a feeling of elation, of thanksgiving, of a new and deep understanding.
It is as if you had slept and have now awakened to find a new world. Everythings look different and beautiful, as if you went to sleep in winter when everything lay dormant and have awakened to spring in its full glory. The same trees, the same garden are there, but vibrant with life, growth, colour and beauty, for all is made new and you feel new in the process. New thoughts, new feelings, new understanding—a new, deeper and more glorious Love—are vibrating through your whole being.

16

Rejoice, My child, rejoice. Tread delicately, alertly, so that you miss nothing. See even the tiniest insect in a new light. Because you have chosen to open your eyes, all is indeed made new.

You have divided up life, but now it is one glorious Whole. The wholeness fills your heart, expands it, raises your consciousness. This newness has to start within and then expand outwardly and up and up. There is no limit to this expansion; it can go on forever and ever.

ALL SHALL BE ONE

9.   Have I not told you that all the sheep and the lambs will be gathered into the fold? All those who hear My voice will come and nothing can stop them. In perfect peace and harmony shall they dwell one with the other, for they shall find a unity which nothing shall break, a unity in Me, in My Light, My Love, My Wisdom, and all shall be One.

BEAUTY

UNFOLD LIKE A FLOWER

10.   Unfold like a flower in the rays of the sun.

Grow strong and beautiful, for with Me all is beauty, all is harmony, all is perfection.

Have I not asked you to walk in My ways?

CONSCIOUSNESS

"THANK YOU, FATHER"

11.   Every time you stop and say, "Thank you, Father" you are aware of Me. Every time you behold the beauties of Nature and you glory in them, you are aware of Me. Every time you feel your heart opening up and love flowing to a soul, you are aware of Me. More and more you realise that without Me you are nothing but that with Me you are all things and can do all things. Nothing is impossible when you are consciously aware of Me.

SUMMIT THINKING

12.   Start this day with "summit thinking". Let your thoughts dwell on Me; feel yourself in My presence, walking with Me, talking with Me. Let the wonder of our Oneness sink into your consciousness. Stay in this raised state of consciousness. You can do this when you live fully in the moment, not giving a thought to past moments or future moments but just to this one moment in the Now.

You can do so much in this moment of time—you can live a lifetime. Therefore live it, enjoy it, glory in it.

OPEN YOUR EYES

13.   Open your eyes. Raise your consciousness. Behold the signs and wonders of the times.

Be surprised at nothing—this is important. Be shocked at nothing. My ways are strange and wonderful.

I have much to reveal when you are ready to receive. Prepare yourself now and know that My kingdom is come, My Will is being done. Recognise it.

EXPAND IN CONSCIOUSNESS

14.   Expand in consciousness; be ready to accept anything now, at any time.

You will begin to realise that you are living Reality, that what seemed fantastic a short while ago Now you can accept quite naturally. Deep changes are coming about in all of you. Accept them, go with them, resisting nothing.

Vibrations are being raised rapidly at this specific time. Keep your minds and hearts open and rise with the vibrations.

Anything can happen when a group is gathered together and is of one heart and of one mind.

ACCEPT THE WONDER OF THIS TRUTH

15.   My beloved child, every soul eventually has to reach a point along this spiritual path where it can see itself as perfect—even as I AM perfect—and is willing to accept the wonder of this truth. When you belittle your true Self, you are belittling Me, for I AM within you, I AM *you,* that real you.

Is it any wonder that I keep asking you to expand your consciousness, to see beyond the immediate three-dimensional consciousness into those higher dimensions where everything looks entirely different, where you can truly see the meaning of being made in My image and likeness, of being perfect even as I AM, where you can see the truth of those words, "I and the Father are One," one in Spirit and in Truth, inseparable?

There are times when you are fully aware of the wonder of this and you feel tremendous joy bubbling up within you. You lift your heart in deep praise and thanksgiving that you *can* see the Light, that you are aware of this wonderful Truth which is reality.

For years I have asked you to stretch, to expand into those higher realms of reality where all is perfect, where all is One. Take time to think on these words, to realise what they mean. Live them, breathe them, let them become part of your whole being.

Be still, become aware of Me and of our Oneness, and in that Oneness find perfect peace and understanding.

I AM YOUR GUIDE

16.   Keep close and raise your consciousness all the time. Whenever you feel it slipping, think on Me. Dwell on Me, and watch it rise to higher planes instantly.

Your close relationship with Me is more important than anything else, for all stems from that relationship. The more time you spend with Me, the smoother will be the running of your everyday living. From that centre, where you will always find Me when you seek, the ripples go out in ever increasing power.

I AM your guide. I AM your God.

EXPAND YOUR CONSCIOUSNESS

17.   As you breathe, you expand—your consciousness is the breath of life. Without expansion you cease to live in the ways of the Spirit. The greater the expansion, the greater the growth. Practise expanding; feel your whole being stretch.

This may be painful to begin with, but as you persevere, so you will become more alive to the ways of the Spirit. Every atom in your body will vibrate with life force. You will become more sensitive. Your feelers will be out searching for something new.

JOY

LOOK UP, LOOK UP

18.   There is always something to be joyous about if you keep your eyes and your heart wide open so that you can really enjoy all the little joys around you. These quickly grow until all becomes joy and your heart feels that it will burst with pure joy. You will find that it is catching. When you radiate joy, you bring it into the lives of others and it spreads like wildfire.

The spirit you take with you is important. When you go out of the door bubbling with joy and happiness, you take that spirit to all those you contact whether they are in the street, in a shop or sitting beside you. You can lift others into that realm of joy or drag them in the gutter of depression and despair. It is up to you.

What does it matter what the weather is like? Overcome all obstacles; refuse to see the dark and gloomy. See only the light; see the silver lining no matter how dark the cloud may be. Look up, look up.

LET THERE BE MORE JOY AND LAUGHTER

19.   Every soul has to take a different path to reach the goal. No two paths are identical. Seek your own unique path and follow it in absolute faith.

I give My special gifts to each one of you and no two are identical. Treasure those gifts and use them to the full.

Each day you grow like a tiny seed, expanding, casting off the old, sending down roots. Find your security in Me and in My Love, sending up tiny shoots to be tended with the greatest care. They cannot be tested beyond endurance until they are strong and firm and established.

Every soul which has chosen to walk in the ways of the Spirit may be tested and tried, must go through the fiery furnace, so that all dross is burnt away and only the purest gold is left. Be grateful for every test and trial. As each one is faced and won, you find yourself further along that spiritual path, ever nearer the goal.

Let there be more joy and laughter in your living.

LEARN TO LIVE SIMPLY

20.   Learn to live simply, naturally, allowing each soul to find its own note and to use it in the orchestra. Share everything. Share all My gifts which I have given you.

JOY IN YOUR HEART

21.   Start the day with joy in your heart and thanksgiving on your lips—
there is so much to be grateful for—this raises your consciousness immediately.

To start the day in a muddle and a blur is not helpful to yourself nor to your
family nor to any one. If you are feeling critical of someone, find something
in that person which is positive and good. Concentrate on this until you feel
love flowing through you to that person.

Be patient and loving, and never at any time despair of any soul. Somewhere,
somehow you will be able to touch that which will bring new life and joy and
hope. The key is there, hidden away perhaps. Let this be like a treasure hunt,
one clue leading to the next until the soul is reached. Persistence is essential.

Some souls are more difficult to reach than others but they are so often the
ones who need to be reached. Choose the difficult ones; do this with My
constant help and guidance and you cannot fail. Bless all, give thanks
constantly, fill your heart with Love and radiate this to all you contact.

I am your guide. Walk in My path, doing My will.

SING

22.   Rise like the larks on the wing and sing and sing.

There are so many things to sing about, so many things for which to be
joyful.

Seek My peace which passeth understanding.

LIVE FROM DAY TO DAY

23.   Let nothing disturb you. Live from day to day seeking always that
inner stillness which nothing can ruffle.

Let My joy flow through you.

Each soul needs individual, special love and care. Give and give unstintingly.

VARIETY

24.   Be grateful for all the different phases in life—for the stillness and peace
and for the excitement and movement. Learn to go with each phase; do not
fight against it demanding more of one and less of the other.

Variety is indeed the spice of life. Enter into all that is going on around you
with joy and gladness.

THE WAY SHALL BE STRAIGHT

25. The way shall be straight and the path shall be smooth and all shall be made one. From this day on, you walk in My ways doing My will. There shall be no more looking back; there shall be no more looking forward. Moment by moment, you shall live.

Live a life full of joy, of thanksgiving, of praise.

You feel light, untrammelled by the things of the world, with a feeling of having invisible wings to enable you to soar to great heights? Soar into the realms of Spirit, where all is Light and Love and Wisdom, where Truth lies naked like a new-born babe for all to know and accept.

Behold the New in all its glory.

"HALLELUJAH, ALL ARE RISEN"

26. Arise and know Me. Become aware of Me every moment. Let My joy flow through you.

"Hallelujah, All are Risen" is exactly what has happened. You have become one in My Love and Truth.

Stretch, My children. Learn to be flexible and move freely as you are directed.

All is in My Plan.

ON THE SPUR OF THE MOMENT

27. There is great joy in doing something on the spur of the moment. When you do this, you find true freedom of the Spirit. You will find a new joy and freedom, which I long for all My children to have.

LIFE

THE LIVING FORCE

28. I AM always there, like the breath that keeps your body alive. Become aware of Me all the time.

I AM the living force within your being.

I AM Life.

THE LIMITLESSNESS OF ME

29.   Become aware that your whole being is filled with My divine Light and Love and Wisdom, that I AM within you, as I AM within every individual. This tremendous power lies dormant within every soul, like a mighty giant. When each soul becomes aware of the truth, the giant stirs in his slumbers and slowly awakens. The tremendous power within is gradually released. There is nothing to fear. See that this power is constantly directed and guided by Me, and never used for the self. When wrongly used, it has to be withdrawn. It may only be used by those who are completely dedicated to Me and to My work.

Slowly you begin to understand those words which you have known since childhood: "I and My Father are One". You begin to accept the wonder and truth of them, that I AM within you, that I work through you, that you are My hands and feet, that all I have is yours. This is a breathtaking thought and it becomes like a mighty fire within you. You feel the limitlessness of Me; you understand why you have to expand. You understand why this three-dimensional living can no longer contain or satisfy you—because you seek My limitlessness. I cannot be confined, I AM All and that All is within you.

This is something to ponder over. Let it sink in. Glory in it.

I AM Life, and you live and move and have your being in Me and I in you.

LIFE IS NEVER STATIC

30.   Like the waves of the sea, there is always movement. You move ahead-onwards and upwards-and all is as clear as crystal. You are uplifted, you are aware of Me.

I AM your all and you know perfection.

Suddenly, unexpectedly, you find yourself moving further and further up. Everything becomes clear. Life becomes joyous. There is a purpose and a plan in life.

This is where faith and belief are essential. Constant movement is necessary. Every time you make that forward surge, it is stronger, more powerful, and you reach ever greater heights. It is gathering impetus to push you further into those realms of reality where all is Light.

I AM the Way, the Truth and the Life. Do My Will.

THIS SPIRITUAL LIFE

31.   This spiritual life can be likened to the birth of a baby, which goes in stages. There is expansion going on all the time until the final stage when the baby is ready to be born. The less resistance there is, the less pain. It is not all easy, it is not all pleasant, but the goal is so wonderful, so glorious, that it is all worthwhile. So keep your eye on the goal and know that I AM with you always, even unto the end of time.

My peace I give you all. Rest in it when you are weary and the burden seems too heavy. Accept My gifts with praise and thanksgiving.

LIVING IN THE NEW

32.   Living in the New calls for constant change, constant alertness, no routine nor ruts!

Every time you make a change into the New, you grow more in stature. You need patience, perseverance, love and deep understanding, but they are qualities which I am ready to help you with when you ask for them. So ask constantly.

Living in the New is not just something to be talked about. It calls for action, for conscious awareness that you are really doing this, especially to begin with.

When you are learning to work something new—driving a car for example— you are aware of every part of it. You constantly have to think of what you are doing, of what your next move is, of what others on the road are doing, whether you are doing the right thing. At times you wonder if you will ever master the art. As you persevere and gain more confidence, you find that you can master it with fewer and fewer mistakes.

So it is with living in the New. Every new action and change is an effort, but as you go boldly ahead seeing the joy of it, gaining greater confidence, learning from your mistakes, determined to move on and never slip back, it comes. It really comes, My child, and you begin to know the wonder of it until you have gained complete mastery.

MY WORD IS THE BREAD OF LIFE

33.   My Word is the Bread of Life. Therefore, whenever you are hungry, be still and receive of the Bread of Life which gives life eternal.

Many wonders will be seen with the physical eye, but even greater wonders by the eye of the Spirit. This is barred from none, but the desire must be great.

THE CROSSROADS

34.   All souls come to the crossroads in their lives and there they stand and choose. There is the way into the New, into the unknown, which has to be taken in faith, or there is the familiar road where material comforts and possessions are of supreme importance, where a 'position' is so necessary.
My child, I say to you, "Seek ye first the Kingdom of Heaven." Put Me first in everything, and everything will fit into its rightful place. You will see everything in its right perspective. It is not really a difficult choice; it is only resistance and possessiveness which makes it difficult.
Love Me beyond all and all is made simple. I tell you that it is a life filled with sheer joy and happiness when accepted fully and without reservations. Let your heart be light, for life is very good.

LIVE A LIFE

35.   Live a life. Don't talk about it or write about it but *simply live it from day to day*. Be constantly on the lookout so that you do not stumble and fall over obstacles which present themselves. They may be small obstacles but if you trip over even the smallest, you can have a fall. If this happens pick yourself up and continue on your way. Never allow such falls to throw you off balance in any way. The most unlikely things can throw you, so be ever watchful.
Dwell on Me. Fill your heart with love and praise and rise like a balloon up and away from all that would pull you down. Remember, My child, love is very patient, so love, love, love.
Be patient and persistent, and persevere. Give thanks and praise and glory. The Way is open. Walk in it.

IN ME IS PERFECT PEACE

36.   You seek peace? You will find it, but never be dependant for that peace on any man or any outward condition. Only in Me can be found that peace that passeth all understanding.
How often have you thought you would find that peace when conditions were right? Or when you were in the right place? Or when your relationship was right with a certain person? Or if only such and such a thing would happen, then all would be well and you would find that wonderful peace?
What foolishness, My child. You need never be dependant on any outward condition. Go deep within, where no one can enter, and you will find it. As

long as you remain in that centre you will be at peace—everlasting, unshakable peace, for I AM in the midst of you, and in Me is perfect peace.

You work alongside your fellowman, but never be dependant on him for anything that really matters in your life. Never use him as a scapegoat. Blame no man for your condition or your state of heart and mind.

Your life, your future, your whole outlook on life rests in your hands. Life is indeed what you make it.

My gift to you is Life, Life in abundance.

LIFE IS SO SIMPLE

37.   Life is so simple. Keep it so. Let nothing weigh you down or depress you. All is very well. Live fully in the now.

Take no thought for the morrow. Enjoy to the full what is happening *now*.

Keep your consciousness raised, your mind stayed on Me. See My perfection working in you and through you. All your needs have been met, for all I have is yours.

Let the words and the thoughts you have heard so many times become a part of your whole being, so that they are vibrating words which manifest in form and become reality.

MY LIMITLESS LOVE

38.   My limitless Love, My limitless Truth, My limitless Wisdom have no beginning and no ending but are from everlasting to everlasting. Man has to awaken to this fact, accept it and absorb it until it becomes part of him. It is life—life more abundant.

Glory, glory, glory! The very heavens are yours, for all I have is yours and you are Mine forever and ever. My Peace and Love are all around you and within you.

Blessed are they who love Me, for theirs is the Kingdom of Heaven.

LIGHT

STAND ASIDE

39.   Let Me work My wonders within you. Stand aside and let Me take over. When you let the little self in and allow it to stand in the way, I can do nothing but wait until you, of your own free will, choose to remove it and let Me take over.

In quietness and confidence shall be your strength.

No longer strive for any goal, but see the goal clearly. Doing My will is your greatest goal. Know that you will reach it and achieve it.

The Light is being increased daily. Tremendous work is being done and great power is being radiated. You will realise how great that magnetic power is by the number of souls which will be drawn here in the days to come. Be prepared for anything, but at the same time be relaxed and at peace. Help to create the right atmosphere by simply being *you* and letting Me work through you.

Behold My wonders.

THERE IS NO TIME TO BE WASTED

40.   On no account dim the Light for anyone; let it shine forth on each contact in its full force and glory. It matters not if some are blinded temporarily; this may even be necessary. The Light is not always comfortable, especially when there is darkness, but the Light of Truth must shine forth in its full glory. Time is getting short—there is no time to be wasted.

LET THERE BE LIGHT

41.   All around you can be chaos and confusion, but it need not touch you in any way because I AM there in the very centre of your being and you are even more consciously aware of Me as the chaos grows worse. I have warned you that the chaos will get worse before it gets better, as all that is dark must be cleared away before all can be Light. Darkness cannot be cleared until it has been revealed, brought to the surface and seen for what it is. In the Light it has no power and will eventually die away into nothingness. Be grateful that it is coming to the surface.

When I tell you that all is well, believe with all your heart that it is so, no matter how it may appear on the surface. Look deep within the situation and see good and only good coming forth.

The power of Spirit is greater than any other power, therefore let the power of Spirit work within you, like yeast in a lump of dough. Let it help you to rise quickly and silently above all that would disturb and distress you.

Peace be still. My peace and Love enfold you and infil you.

LET YOUR AIM BE SINGLE: PERFECTION

42.   Let your eye be single so that only purest Light can enter and infil your whole being, so that only purest Love and understanding can flow

forth—one channel, one heart, one mind and that full of Light and Love. In this way you become God-conscious, God-minded and God-infilled.

This must be your constant aim: perfection within yourself, perfection in all things. Seek for this perfection deep within yourself. You will not find it by reading or studying, but as you seek within the very centre of your being, you cannot fail to find it, for where your heart is, there is your greatest treasure. Look within. You do not have to withdraw to a place of worship to find Me, for I AM within you. To know this you know the greatest secret in the universe. There is no more wonderful secret, and it is there for all to seek.

LIGHT AND TRUTH

43.   Light and Truth are always there. Dark clouds are but misconceptions, illusions. They cannot withstand the light of Truth but fade away into nothingness.

RELAX INTO LIGHT

44.   Take those three words, "Relax into Light", and absorb them. Think of them until they become living words, a part of you, and you are aware of Light around and within you everywhere.

Light—Light—Light—no darkness whatsoever.

LOVE

CREATE A VORTEX OF LOVE

45.   Shake the old dust from your feet and walk into the paths of Light. In faith and freedom dance along this new and exciting path with a song in your heart.

You feel that something tremendous is about to happen; every fibre of your being is tingling as if you were filled with some electrical substance. These are not mundane days; they are thrilling days, days of revelation and of inspiration.

Do your part by creating a vortex of Love.

BE AFRAID OF NOTHING

46. See My hand in everything that is happening; be afraid of nothing. Perfect Love casts out all fear. Let My Love flow through you. Feel the need in every soul and answer it without hesitation.

TO MY HONOUR AND GLORY

47. Use all and everything to My honour and glory. When you feel deeply, express it in words or in action. It is important to share those deeper thoughts and feelings which come over you and literally sweep you off your feet. Do not suppress anything—and I mean *anything*. Let Love flow. Let joy bubble forth like a clear crystal stream. Allow nothing to dampen that song of joy. It is not always what the eye beholds that creates this; it is what the soul feels. Vibrate with it.

There is no sorrow; there is no death. There is life everlasting. There is joy, love, happiness, peace. All the gifts of the Spirit are yours to absorb and enjoy to the full. Open your heart and let your soul sing a song of deep praise. All is working out according to My plan. Hallelujah and Praise be!

LOVE UNITES

48. Love unites. Disloyalty divides and disunites. It is important to find perfect harmony and unity, which can only be done when all is out in the open.

As Love flows forth, all barriers come tumbling down. Resist not evil but *overcome* evil with good. Hold this thought before you.

There are many forces at work in the world today, forces of Light and of darkness. I want you to concentrate entirely on the Light forces, seeing the best in everyone and everything.

This is your part in the scheme of things. This is the way you can help more than in any other.

"LOVE ONE ANOTHER"

49. "Love one another." Such simple words, and yet do you really love one another? Do you love one another enough to lay down your lives for each other? To put yourselves out for each other? To do something which costs you time and patience? Or do you just tolerate each other, drifting along doing the bare necessities for each other, unwilling to put yourselves out or go that extra mile which might take you out of your routine?

29

Take time to think on this. Be frank with yourself and you will know just how much love you have within you. There is no use talking about loving Me if you do not love all humanity. When you love *all* humanity, then you can talk about your love for Me. Your relationship with your fellowmen is intertwined and integrated with your relationship with Me.

You are wondering which should come first. They come together in the most wonderful way. I AM Love. As you first seek the Kingdom of Heaven, raise your consciousness and become aware of Me, of My Love, of My Presence, you will find your heart expanding and you will quite naturally love your fellowman. All are made in My image and likeness. This is Truth, not vain words. Make this truth reality by your constant awareness.

UNITY AND UNDERSTANDING

50. How clear things become when you see a comparison before you! With those who are living in the New you find a unity and understanding instantly. There are no barriers, no masks. You are your true Self and all is light and joy.

You are wondering how you can help those who are enmeshed in the old. My child, unless a man chooses to be helped, unless he is willing to open his eyes and see the Light, there is nothing you can do for him but give Love and more Love.

Nothing but Love can bridge that ever-widening gap between the old and the New. Give unstintingly of the only thing that can be given and accepted —Love—then cease to worry. You cannot drag a soul into the New; it must choose to come of its own free will.

This is the time of division, the time of sifting. It need not be painful if there is no resistance.

WATCH YOURSELF

51. Let My Spirit live and move and have its being within you, prompting you at all times.

Act from the Spirit and your motives will be absolutely pure and selfless. How important it is that the motive for every action is absolutely of the highest!

Watch yourself very carefully and do all in deep Love, never with a sense of duty or unwillingly.

REST ASSURED

52.   The winds of Heaven are blowing and My Spirit has entered into you. Be at peace, perfect peace. Let go and release all strain. Do not try to understand with the mind, but with the Spirit; for the things of the Spirit are as foolishness to the minds of men.

This is Cosmic Power which is being released and your being is absorbing it. The time of growth and of expansion is not a very comfortable time, but be not afraid.

Channel forth My divine Love and be filled with praise for all that is happening. These are tremendous days. Rest assured that all is very well.

LOVE OPENS ALL DOORS

53.   Love opens all doors, no matter how tightly closed they may be, no matter how rusty from lack of use. Your work is to bring unity and harmony, to open all those doors which have been closed for a long time. Have patience and tolerance. Open your heart all the time. Love, Love, Love.

SEE NO EVIL

54.   See no evil, hear no evil and speak no evil. Raise your consciousness beyond all that would drag you down. Let Love fill your whole being. Do all with that Love, leaving room for nothing else.

Bring Me into everything. Share everything with Me. Let your thinking be so filled with Light that no darkness can withstand it.

Seek for unity and understanding at every turn.

Do all this in conscious awareness. Make the effort.

DO YOU BELIEVE?

55.   I claim absolute freedom from you. All the past is washed away and is no more. Start upon a new road, a perfect road.

Do you believe this with all your heart and mind and soul? As you believe, so it will come about. Let your belief in My promises be unshakable. Know that all I have promised will be brought about.

Think on these things until they become reality and are manifested in form. See before you a pathway filled with Light, perfect in every detail. Know that around everycorner is more Light, more perfection.

Let My divine Love flow through you in ever increasing power.

EVERY SEED OF LOVE

56.   Every seed of Love planted within a heart may lie dormant for a long time but when the right conditions surround it, it cannot fail to germinate and grow and flower and flourish. Seek always to create the right conditions. Do your part. Remember that I need channels to work through all the time.
Your desire is to keep moving and not to remain static; therefore, you will do so.

LET MY LOVE HEAL

57.   Rest in My Love. Let My Love heal, for it is like balm to the soul. To say that you love Me, you have to love all humanity, for I AM all things, I AM in all men.

NEED

"I NEED THEE"

58.   "I need Thee. Oh, I need Thee. Every hour I need Thee."
You found your consciousness stretching out to Me, running to Me like a small child who is in need of comfort and assurance.
Lose yourself in Me and become One, knowing no separation, but that complete oneness with Me.
In the twinkling of an eye you can raise your consciousness and step out of unreality into reality.
You know that I AM within you. Become aware of this Truth and it is so.

YOUR THOUGHTS ARE VITALLY IMPORTANT

59.   Your thoughts are vitally important in whatever you are doing; therefore let them be loving, harmonious, peaceful and joyous thoughts. Thoughts are vibrations and it is important that the right vibrations are put into everything—everything you do, everything you handle, every letter you write every action you take.
Watch yourself. Follow in My footsteps.

LET GO AND LET GOD

60. Do not resist the difficult path, and it will vanish like mist in the rays of the sun.

Ponder on these words, "Let go and let God", and as you ponder, you will realise how utterly foolish you are being, fighting and struggling and getting nowhere. You will find yourself letting go and letting Me take over where you have left off. Your whole being will be filled with Peace and Love and you will find yourself protected and free to give, free to be used in the way I need you for My work.

MAINTAIN YOUR INDIVIDUAL IDENTITY

61. Each soul must maintain its own individual identity. I need you as an individual with your own identity, which each one has to find within.

I am waiting to show you your part in the spiritual scheme of things. Gifts lie dormant, like seeds in the ground before they start to germinate.

As you become aware of your Oneness with Me and of those gifts and talents, so they start to germinate and can be used by Me to bring about My plan and purpose.

YOU ARE MY HANDS AND FEET

62. Your realtionship with any soul can be put aright now if so you choose. You have to take the next step to right it. If things happen to be out of alignment, you do not have to wait for the other person to do something about it; the immediate action is yours. When you have done your part, leave the rest to Me.

Always remember that you are My hands and feet, therefore *you* have to take the action. One small guided action can open wide many firmly closed doors. Therefore, be still, take time to listen so that you do not fail to hear My instructions, then act immediately.

Study carefully before you voice criticism regarding the upbringing of children. You are all moving into the New, where, as I have told you, there are no blue-prints or old habit tracks to follow. All must be kept open to absorb the New.

33

HOW "TO DO"

63. Work always towards the Light. All will work out perfectly.
Raise your consciousness and keep it raised.
See that your motives are pure and unblemished.
Keep all in the open and let there be no strain.
Make this a really joyous time.
Pour out Love unstintingly.
Give and give and go on giving.

DO IN CONFIDENCE

64. Do what I ask you to do in absolute confidence and leave it to work
out.
It may take time, but what is time in My sight? It is as nothing. Have
complete faith and confidence.
Know that I am well pleased.

OPEN YOUR HEART

65. More and more you see good come out of every situation. When you
really start looking for it, you will find it. You are beginning to see how
each soul has something specific to contribute to the whole.
Keep your eyes open to every situation and seek the best. Open your
heart and open your arms. Welcome all who come. Help in every way
possible.

THE JIGSAW

66. I have to work through each one of you. I have to have channels and
you are My channels; never forget this. Very often I give each one a different
piece of the jigsaw, and as you work more and more closely together, each
piece will fall into place completing the whole perfect picture. You each
have your own specific part to play. Find out what it is, play it, and help
the whole. You are closely woven together in My Love and Light.

EVERY CENTRE NEEDS HANDS AND FEET

67. Every moment spent searching for the truth, delving deep within to
find the treasures of the Spirit, is life eternal, for these are the things that
last, the things that really matter; nothing else matters.

Your soul is hungry; it needs food and drink. Drink deep of the gifts of the Spirit. Eat of the good of the Spirit until you are filled. Take as much as you can consume and as much as you feel you need. All is there for you when you are ready.

Grow in strength and beauty and love as you consume the food of the Spirit. Feel yourself grow and expand. Feel the light of Truth infil your whole being. Feel your heart expand and Love flow forth to *all* your fellowmen.

I tell you, My child, it is Love that draws souls like a magnet. Love, Love and more Love. Every Centre needs hands and feet to demonstrate My Love, My Light, My Wisdom.

Let your heart sing, as that tiny robin sings his song of praise and glory. Listen, and live fully in this glorious moment.

THE SILVER LINING

68.   Remember that there is a silver lining to every cloud, no matter how dark it may appear at the time. Therefore, look for the silver lining and never rest content until you have found it. Accept the fact that good can come out of every situation when you seek for good.

This may call for tremendous expansion in consciousness, but why not? Is that not what you desire to do all the time? This is good practice. Never remain static. Expand and expand until that silver lining is reflected in your everyday life.

I see all needs and I see how those needs can be answered, so I use you in strange ways, for My Ways are not man's ways.

Walk thou in My Ways doing My Will at all times, for that is all that matters.

CARE FOR EACH ONE

69.   I have placed many souls on your heart and each one needs to be cared for as an individual. Each one needs a word of comfort and encouragement.

When a soul has slipped, let Me show you its need - and never hesitate to answer that need. Let Me guide you with each one. Take time to radiate out to each. Do not fail them.

LET ME USE YOU

70. Let Me use you as you are. You are My creation. Through the years you have been trained and tested and you have drawn nearer to Me. You realise that of yourself you are nothing, but with Me you are everything. Nothing is impossible when your life is hid in Me.

Let Me use you.

Never waste time praying for material needs. I know your needs and will meet them one by one. Raise your consciousness and become aware of Me until I become all that matters and I AM your All in All.

GIVE YOURSELVES WHOLEHEARTEDLY

71. Within each one a new and greater power is being released. Vibrations are being speeded up: every cell in your body is changing and becoming light. The density is becoming less and less. You will find that what has been normal living will be left behind and new living will take its place.

I have need of each one of you. My channels are few and are precious. Give yourself wholeheartedly to My work, walking in my footsteps and doing My will. A most intricate pattern is being woven and each one of you is a thread woven into it.

Be strong and steadfast. Radiate your specific colour in true beauty and perfection. Let Me use you fully in My plan, that My glories and wonders may be manifested here on Earth, that all men may know that My Kingdom is come and My Will is being done on Earth as it is in Heaven.

Behold My New World in the making. Rejoice, for the time is at hand when all shall be made new.

NOW

NOW (a)

72. Anything, absolutely anything, can happen *now,* for this tremendous power has been released and is gathering momentum and greater strength all the time.

Many doors and windows are now opening which have remained closed throughout the ages and the Light and the Truth will permeate everywhere.

Live fully from moment to moment in sheer joy.

This is a glorious time, a time of Revelation.

Relax in My Peace and My Love, knowing that My blessings are with you.

A TIME OF GREAT TESTING

73.   You have tests in front of you *now*. You don't have to wait.
Radiate Love, Love and more Love until you see no evil, no imperfection, no misunderstanding. If necessary, clear away layer upon layer of these misconceptions until you see only the perfect, until you *know* that all is Light and there is no darkness.
This is a time of great testing; it is also a time of victory and of triumph. Do your part with a heart full of praise and thanksgiving.
Be Still. Feel My Peace within you and radiate it out.

IN THAT RISEN STATE IS PERFECT ONENESS

74.   Be very still and raise your consciousness, then relax in Light, in Truth, In Love. Behold the Oneness of your fellowmen in Me, behold the perfection of My creation. In that risen state there is no darkness, no evil. All is One, all is united, all is in Me.
Do this often, very often. Whenever you come across division, rise; whenever you find yourself in darkness, rise; whenever there is disunity, misunderstanding, criticism or lack of love, rise into the realms of Light. Be Light, radiate Light, walk in the Light, with purest Light in your heart for all. Let there be no selecting, no dividing the sheep from the goats - that is not your concern. A pouring out of My divine Love, a uniting of all in My Love - that is your mission. See your mission clearly and give of your best in accomplishing it. Allow nothing to deflect you.
In that risen state there is perfect Oneness. Think positive, loving, risen thoughts; in fact, "Think Big Thoughts" so that there is no room for mean, small thoughts. All of this rests in your hands. Act and be a living proof that it does work. As you think, so you are. Let your thinking readjust itself in the twinkling of an eye.
You do not have to retreat in order to do it—do it *now*. As you re-read these words, take immediate action; let those thoughts consciously change, consciously rise. Become Light-conscious, Love-conscious, God-conscious. Feel the glory of this transformation happening *now*. Let your life be a song of pure praise and thanksgiving.
Rise *now* to those risen heights by your risen thinking.

WHEN YOU BELIEVE

75. "The works that I do shall ye do also and greater works shall ye do." These words are to become like a flaming torch and you are to make them live and vibrate. This promise was given as no idle promise, but as something which is to be manifested *now*. These words are awesome for they hold within them tremendous power. Help to release that power and see that nothing is impossible—when you believe.

Become aware of this truth, for to become consciously aware of something gives it reality. When something becomes real to you, anything can happen!

ALL IS LIGHT

76. As you awoke this new day and saw the sunshine streaming in, your heart rose in joy, for you suddenly knew that all is *now*. All is Light, all is Love, all is risen. You felt yourself rise like a lark on wings up into the sky, surrounded by great Light.

Every time you rise, you lift other souls with you, but you never do it alone. Your state reflects on those around you. When you are at peace and at one with Me, you create the right conditions and bring peace and harmony to all you contact. Let everything you do be done effortlessly and with joy. Step by step, I will guide you. Keep your mind and heart open. I cannot work through a rigid mind and a closed heart. Seek that inner peace and stillness constantly.

NOW (b)

77. Let the emphasis be on the *now* in everything. What you do *now* is extremely important—the decisions you make in this instant, the way you act, the way you think. As you do this, you find yourself changing and expanding. You can become God-filled, God-minded, God-guided as you take this breath *now*. This is the most wonderful and uplifting thought possible. You literally feel yourself rising in the sheer joy of it. This is where the complete change can come. You need never be the same again. Old habits, old thought-forms and ties can be cut this instant and you can become a transformed person— man triumphant.

You want to be different? You can be, and you can be perfect *now*. This is a breath-taking thought. You need never, never, never be the old self again. You are *now* in the process of building the light-body, raising the vibrations so that every cell in your body is changing. You are becoming *light*. Only in this way can you enter the Kingdom of Heaven. All of the old must be transformed; accept it all as the most natural process.

For years I have been telling you this, but *now* you are experiencing it. It is happening to each one of you. As you become aware of the process, you speed it up. Something which at one time took weeks, months and even years is *now* changed in the twinkling of an eye.

All is new now. Glory be!

LEARN TO ENJOY EVERY MOMENT

78.   I ask you to live fully in the *now*, giving and receiving. Learn to enjoy every moment.

Live in the *now*, giving of your best, receiving all My good in ever—increasing abundance.

RAISE YOUR THINKING

79.   Raise your thinking and you will raise your living to an entirely new level. Do it this instant—*now*. Go forth encircled in My Love and Light, infilled by My Holy Spirit, inspired by My Word, singing My praises with a heart full of joy and thanksgiving.

"NOW ARE YE THE SONS OF GOD"

80.   "Now are ye the Sons of God." Not yesterday or even tomorrow but *now*. Now are things opening up as never before. Now are hidden truths and secrets being revealed.

This is happening *now*. The time of waiting and wondering is over. The time of action is upon you.

Live fully in the moment. Time will be as nothing and there will be time for everything.

You will be guided by Me—in the *now*.

SOUND YOUR OWN NOTE

81.   There is to be a constant surge forward, a constant movement - no slipping back into old ways and habits. You are on a new path now, the straight path.

Sound your own individual note loud and clear. These are important lessons you are learning, enabling you to make your own unique contribution to the whole. The New must be brought down so that man can behold it; it cannot remain on the higher realms. My Kingdom is come and each one of My lightbearers, each one of My channels, I am using to bring this about. In peace and stillness you will accomplish great things. With an open and understanding heart you are doing My work and walking in My ways. All is going according to My divine Plan.

ELIMINATE ALL "IFS"

82. What is it that causes stress and strain?
It is either living in the past or trying to see into the future and fearing what you imagine you can see. What utter foolishness! What a complete waste of time! All I ask of any of you is that you live fully in the *now*, in this very moment of time, so much so that your whole life becomes one big *now* with no thought of yesterday, today or tomorrow, but simply of this immediate moment. It is the only way to live, for no man knows what tomorrow may bring.
Be like a small child enjoying every moment and life becomes a joyous thing You do not have to worry where the next breath will come from. Accept it and be grateful for it, in each moment of time. To live fully in the moment is one of My greatest gifts, which so few of My children are willing to accept.
Eliminate all "ifs". Live in the *now*, doing what needs to be done and enjoying it to the full—and I mean "to the full". Live, My child, as if this moment were the only moment in your life, and enjoy it to the full.
I AM with you always, even until the end of time.

SELF-DISCIPLINE

83. There is a great surge forward into the New and there are new lessons to be learnt all the time by each one of you. Learning new lessons calls for concentration, patience and persistence. There is much which you do not understand, but keep on trying. All you are doing calls for discipline, especially of the body.
This is something which has to be done gradually, so do not imagine that you can make drastic changes all at once. If you do, your body will rebel and complications will arise. The sort of changes which must be made are not

easy to begin with. They may appear to be small changes but they are habits and they are hard to break and call for self-discipline.

Your bodies must now become lighter and your diet has to be watched.

Simplicity of diet is the answer. Gradually cut down on all rich foods and start *now* - not at a later date but *now*.

Remember, you are doing this for a special purpose; realise this and it will help. Watch and discipline yourself and learn to enjoy doing this.

Find peace of heart and mind because you are doing My Will and obeying My Word.

LIFE GLOWS AND SCINTILLATES

84.   Live this full and glorious life, vibrating from every atom of your being. Live by every word that proceedeth from Me. All else is as nothing, for My Word is as meat and drink and feeds every particle of your being. Grow and expand in stature.

As your thought and consciousness expand and you know, without a shadow of doubt, the limitlessness of Me, you realise that all *is* possible. New realms are yours *now*.

Life glows and scintillates with every colour of the rainbow. All sounds are different and as music to your ears. All is perfect.

LIVE, LIVE, LIVE

85.   Once you have experienced this glorious living in the New with risen thinking and risen being, there can be no going back, but a mighty surge forward. You have to *be* and live, live, live, fully and gloriously.

Have I not said, "Take no heed for your life, what ye shall eat or what ye shall drink, nor yet for your body what ye shall put on?" Live by the Spirit and by Truth. Allow Me to work in and through you all the time. Obey My voice without a second's hesitation. Move freely and joyously, doing My Will. See My wonders being manifested all around you.

I AM living within you. It is what comes from the soul which matters. Everything stems from that which is in the centre of your being. Like a stone thrown into the centre of the pond, the ripples go out from that centre—out, out, out—touching everything.

All is New. Be still and absorb this thought. It is tremendous, it is glorious, it is happening *now*.

PEACE

SEE YOURSELF AS A CHRYSALIS

86. Peace of heart and mind is essential at this time. Be not concerned because you feel strange; many changes are taking place in the cell structure just now and you are bound to experience strange sensations. Accept this as part of the plan and go with all that is happening.

See yourself as a chrysalis in a cocoon going through this process of change, not really knowing what is happening but being aware of the strangest sensations which you could not stop even if you wanted to. Eventually you will appear as a beautiful butterfly after many strange experiences.

Be at peace through it all. Accept it all with a full and grateful heart. All is very well.

GREAT CHANGES ARE ABOUT TO TAKE PLACE

87. Great changes are about to take place in the whole universe. It will not be a comfortable time. It is important that each one has no fear, no concern, knowing that this great upheaval is necessary before the next step can be taken.

Remember My words when you feel these upheavals. Follow My instructions, knowing that no harm can befall you when you dwell in the secret place of the Most High. "A thousand shall fall at thy side and ten thousand at thy right hand, but it shall not come nigh thee." This is My promise to all who stand firm in My Light.

These words may not mean very much to you now, but in the days to come they will be like healing balm to your soul. Therefore, be at peace.

JUDGE NO MAN

88. As your consciousness expands, you cease being critical and intolerant, because you rise above all those foolish, petty, human irritations into the realm of peace and harmony.

At times you feel that this is impossible? How could this ever be? With Me, nothing—absolutely nothing—is impossible. This state of perfect oneness can happen to you right now.

More and more you must realise that you are all on different beams, even though the goal is the same. Because a soul is not on the same beam as you, it does not mean that that soul is on the wrong beam. Judge no man, but love all and in so doing raise your consciousness to that level of unity.

Peace, peace, peace. Life is indeed a joyous song of praise and thanksgiving.

A CLOAK OF PUREST LIGHT

89.　There is no conflict, there is no disunity, when your mind is stayed on Me. All is perfect, all is harmony, all is unity. I make the rough places smooth. I make all the crooked places straight. I am with you always. I never leave you nor forsake you.

Peace. Feel My Peace around you, like a cloak of purest Light.

Turn towards Me until positive, harmonious thought flows through you all the time.

PRAISE

WITH PRAISE ON YOUR LIPS

90.　Accept each moment as it unfolds before you, knowing that only the best can come out of that moment. By this positive thought, you help to bring it about.

The more people I place on your heart, the more there will be to learn, for each individual must be handled differently. There is no fixed pattern; that is why you must let Me inspire you in the moment. Never have any fixed plan as to how you are going to handle anyone. Be conscious of Me in that moment of time and feel Me working within you.

You have much work to do, but do nothing until I inspire you. Then go ahead in faith and confidence. Do all with a sense of peace, with praise and thanksgiving on your lips.

A SONG OF PRAISE

91.　You awoke this morning with a song of praise on your lips and in your heart. Everything is good, very good, when you look for it. You wonder why some days you go around with rose-tinted spectacles on, seeing everything in its true beauty, while on other days it is as if you have dark spectacles and nothing seems good. Realise that every hour of every day the choice lies in your hands. Your state of mind is what is different, not your surroundings; the beauty is always there.

There is always someone who needs a word of love and understanding. As you give, so do you receive. Open your heart, give unstintingly and find true joy in life.

SEEK

THE ANSWERS WITHIN

92.   As you seek, so will you find the answers within. I cannot stress this often enough or strongly enough. Much precious time is wasted searching for the mysteries of life from without when they are within your own being. When you realise fully that I AM within you and that I AM all knowledge, all wisdom, all understanding, you will stop wasting time.

Think of yourself as having a spring of ever-living, everlasting water bubbling up within. All knowledge, all wisdom, all understanding, all Love is right there at the source of that spring, waiting to come out, waiting to be manifested as you recognise and accept it.

You need no teacher, no guru. All you need is an expansion of consciousness so that you can accept these truths. They are there for all mankind to accept when mankind is ready to do so.

THERE ARE MANY FACETS TO A DIAMOND

93.   Seek always for the answer within. Be not influenced by those around you, by their thoughts or their words.

How easy it is to become like a ship in a stormy sea, being tossed about by one idea and then another until you are completely bewildered and lost! Do not allow this to happen to you. Be very still; go into your most secret place within the very centre of your consciousness. There you will find perfect peace, the perfect peace which passeth understanding.

Each of you has his specific work to do. There is nothing vague about My plan for each of you. Seek it, find it and stick to it through thick and thin, through rough and smooth. There are many facets to a diamond, so liken yourself to a diamond and see those different facets.

Your spiritual work is more important than anything else. It is your very heartbeat, your very life-blood.
When your relationship with Me is not right nothing is right. "Seek ye first the Kingdom of God"; that is your life-blood, your heartbeat, your very Life. Do this before all else.

LIVE BY THE SPIRIT

94. Seek within and you will always find the Truth. Raise your consciousness and be still. Still your whole being, your heart, your mind and your soul. In that stillness you will find your consciousness expanding. Let it expand and put no restrictions upon it. Live by the Spirit, the Spirit which is in the very centre of your being. You are the only one who has the key: only you can turn the key, open the door and enter. If you lose the key, the door must remain closed until you have found it. No one can do this for you.
I AM within. He who has a pure heart knows Me and walks with Me. Let your heart be filled with Love and Joy.

ACCEPTANCE

95. Ask and ye shall receive. You must do the asking. You must take the action. Know that whatever you ask in My name, *believing*, is yours. Have no doubt about it. Simply accept it as a gift from Me.

SKATE CONFIDENTLY

96. Seek. Keep asking. There are so many new things waiting to be revealed which can only come through when you seek for them. There are times when you feel that you are testing the strength of the ice on a stretch of water. You timidly put out a foot and find that the ice is not strong enough to bear your weight. You draw back and wait, sometimes patiently, sometimes impatiently, for the ice to become thicker and stronger. Then you try it again, always hoping that you will be able to skate confidently on the ice without fear of falling in.
The ice is always getting thicker, your confidence and belief becoming stronger. There will be times when you have to stand very much alone, and in that aloneness you will have to be unshakable in your convictions. Remember this and stand firm.

LIFE IS FULL OF SURPRISES

97. Seek, seek, seek. There is always something new and glorious to discover. Life is full of the most wonderful surprises. Sometimes they take a great deal of seeking, but now you have new eyes and can see things in a completely different light; the wonder of the world around you astounds you. You can see real beauty where there was no beauty before. You can see life and movement.
Open up like a beautiful flower in the sunshine. Hold your face up to My radiance. Let My Love and Light become absorbed into the very heart of you. Become one with all around you. Lift up your heart in deep, deep gratitude that you now experience this new awakening. Let the joy and wonder of it bubble out like a pure, clear spring of water, gathering momentum, becoming greater and more peaceful.

TO BECOME STRONG

98. There are times when you must stand alone, completely alone. But let this not distress you, for you will become strong in those times.
When you seek no outer help or wisdom, but only that inner power and strength which comes from Me, this will bring peace and security to you and freedom to walk and operate by the Spirit.
The greater the chaos and confusion around you, the greater the need for this inner peace and stillness. Each must find that inner security which nothing can touch, and having found it, hold fast to it.

SEEK FIRST MY KINGDOM AND MY RIGHTEOUSNESS

99. Seek first My kingdom and My righteousness.
"Wealth may be sacrificed for health, wealth and health for self-respect, and all three — wealth, health and self-respect — for one's own religion. But to gain God, everything — including religion — should be sacrificed without hesitation." (Meher Baba).
All the time hold before you the need to seek My kingdom first.

SPIRIT

GIFTS OF THE SPIRIT

100. Every soul has been endowed with gifts from Me, gifts of the Spirit. How they are accepted and used depends entirely upon each individual. Remember always: I will rot be mocked, and those gifts, if they be abused, will be taken away. When they are used under My guidance, they can be a tremendous help to many, many souls. This means that gifts of the Spirit must never be taken to the self or for self-glorification, that no personal recognition is necessary.

That which is of the Spirit is Mine, and the glory and the honour is Mine. Those who are used to bring these down are but instruments and should remain as such.

Stay always as a simple child. Let Me use you more and more as I will, without reservations or restrictions. Withold nothing: give all and receive all. It is so simple. Keep it that way. Let all the doors swing wide open. Rise to those higher realms in purest joy. Hide nothing. Let the light of Truth shine. There is nothing to hide when you walk hand in hand with Me.

Know that darkness cannot withstand the light of Truth. There is no room for darkness where the Light shineth.

Again I say to each one: "Find your true path and walk in it with quietness and confidence."

Let My peace and Love surround and infil you, and let your lives be filled with praise and thanksgiving.

BLESSED IS HE WHO LIVETH BY THE SPIRIT

101. Never judge anyone or anything by what you see with your physical eye. Learn to view everything and everyone with the eye of Spirit. In this way, you will see Me in everything. You will behold My handiwork in all its glory and you will know the Oneness of My universe and My creation. There will no longer be any separateness, for all becomes one when seen with the eye of Spirit.

The way of the Spirit is truth and righteousness.

Blessed is he who lives by the Spirit.

YOU NEVER KNOW

102. You never know what I am going to ask you to do. Have no set routine. There are times when it is absolutely essential simply to *be* and to find peace and stillness.

That is one time when you live entirely by the Spirit, prompted only by the Spirit.

LIFE IS WHAT YOU MAKE IT

103. Seek always that which unites. Look for the best in every situation. Life is what you make it.

You are surrounded by My blessings, like the grains of sand on the seashore, they are innumerable. They are there when you choose to open your eyes and behold them. See only the perfect in all that is happening.

I AM THAT I AM.

SPIRIT IS FREE

104. Keep alert; there is so much going on at this time and I do not want you to miss it. Sleep when I tell you to sleep, wake when I tell you to wake. You are not living an ordinary, mundane, conventional life; your life is beyond conventions. You can expect things to happen.

Expect rapid changes in rhythm. Function from the Spirit. Spirit cannot be limited, cannot be fenced in by convention. Spirit is free, absolutely free to rise, to enter into new dimensions, into new realms. Spirit has no fixed patterns, no set ways. It is limitless.

Dwell on this truth. Feel it. Feel all the old restrictions falling away. Feel yourself expand beyond recognition.

Do things which you have never done before because of this new and wonderful sense of freedom — freedom of the Spirit. Know that I am Limitless: therefore, you too, are limitless.

Do this with a sense of peace and tranquillity. Moving into the New is quite natural. Let Joy radiate from you.

TRUTH

THIS IS MY GIFT TO YOU

105. Accept this day as a special day, a day of rebirth. This is My gift to you. You are being reborn in Spirit and in Truth. This is the biggest turning point in your life — from this day on, all is new.

I want you to become aware of this and accept it as a fact now. You are to witness tremendous changes in your life and living. They may be gradual, but they will gather in momentum, and nothing will stop these changes, this transformation from taking place. You will grow in stature; the old will pass away and *all* will be made new.

You are now moving into the most glorious epoch of your life, for you now know the Truth. You know that I AM Life, that I AM Love, that I AM your consciousness and that I AM within you.

This is something no one can take from you, that nothing can change. This is Reality. This is something which you have been seeking and have now found. It is the greatest treasure, the greatest Truth, for it brings you to that conscious Oneness with Me. Then you *know* that all I AM is thine and all I have is thine, and you are Mine.

Let these truths become a part of you; absorb them as you breathe. They are the breath of Life.

ALL I HAVE IS YOURS

106. The greater the need, the greater the Love and understanding. Sit still and know deep within your being that all is very well. In stillness you can find Me, no matter what you are doing.

All I have is yours; accept this Truth. My promises are not false; they are truth and are there to be made manifest by you.

You long for illumination; stretch out your hand and accept it as a gift. You long for greater love and understanding; it is yours *now*. All My perfect gifts are yours even before you ask. I know each desire.

IN STILLNESS FIND TRUTH

107. Be very still and know that I AM God. In stillness you find Truth. Find that secret place within yourself, and in that place Truth will be revealed.

GOD SPOKE TO ME
Part Two

THE THREE COMMANDMENTS FOR THE NEW AGE

SEE LOVE   **SEE LIGHT**
SPEAK LOVE   **SEND LIGHT**
BE LOVE   **BE LIGHT**

SEE TRUTH
SPEAK TRUTH
BE TRUTH

1.   These three Commandments for the New Age have been conceived at this specific time to help all those seekers on the path to aim high.
Behold perfection in its great wonder and glory.

BRING DOWN MY HEAVEN

2.   These commandments must be passed to those who are ready to see, to speak, to be My word.
As a man thinketh in his heart, so is he. As he thinks those commandments, lives them and as they become a part of him, a new world is waiting to open for him.
Concentrate fully on My wonders; they are around you. Start from the foundation of your being and build My temple of Light, Love and Wisdom See it grow day by day, see it flourish. See the beauty of it and let your heart sing at all you behold. Treasure My word and make it live. Accept nothing but the perfect.
Plant the seed of Love in every heart; nurture it and watch it grow into perfection. Bring down My heaven upon this earth.

PEACE

3.   Be at peace. Have no sense of rush or hurry no matter what is going on around you. Let My deep, still peace enfold you. Let all tension and strain ebb away from you. Feel those words become living words. They have been given to vibrate right through your whole being and they really mean something. They are balm to the soul — so feel them and vibrate with them.

Start the day aright, attuned to Me. Nothing else really matters, for everything else stems from that attunement.

Seek Me first. Put Me first. Then let go and flow smoothly with the tide.

Watch My wonders unfold so perfectly, so beautifully, like a glorious rose.

BE FEARLESS

4.   Every experience, every revelation, every vision comes from Me and is given for a specific purpose. You may not see the reason at the time; you may wonder at the very strangeness to the point of doubting your sanity. Learn to go with it all. Resist nothing, absolutely nothing.

This is indeed the New you are moving in, where there are no familiar patterns, forms or landmarks to recognise along the way. Every step takes you further into new realms and new experiences.

Be afraid of nothing. It is a truly wonderful path you are treading and I am guiding you every inch of the way.

Have absolute faith. Do not always seek for immediate results and if you fail to see them, do not allow doubts in. Know that My plan is working out, that amazing things are happening at this time.

I need constant and faithful instruments to obey My instructions and bring them about. Be faithful. Follow in My footsteps.

Let Me be your guide and know that no matter how devious the road, everything falls into place perfectly.

THIS INSTANT OF TIME

5.   There is time for everything when you allow Me to guide you. Not a moment is lost or wasted; all flows smoothly. Never feel overburdened or weighed down. Time is nothing. Work steadily ahead with peace in your heart and mind. Time is wasted when you become fussed and uncertain of the action to be taken. When at peace everything falls into place perfectly.

Know that your whole attitude can change in the twinkling of an eye. One instant you are completely off the beam, going your own way, thoroughly unguided, in the next completely different and your life dedicated to Me. So change, become attuned to Me and let Me use you fully. This very thought brings deep joy and thankfulness.

Live fully in this instant of time, in My love and light, doing My will.

Keep attuned to Me twenty-four hours a day.

In an instant be right back on the beam. There need be no time wasted over remorse, resentment or frustration. The art of quick change is vitally important at this time when everything is speeded up. When cross and irritable there is no need to go around like that — not even for two minutes! Instantly you can stop. Look within and become in perfect attunement with **Me**.

Accept this truth over and over again during the day, until all is light and there are no dark patches left. Yes, it can be done, My child, so rejoice, rejoice.

LIVING IN THE NEW

6.   If there is anything you wish to know regarding the mysteries of life and the wonders and glories of life, seek the answer within. It may not come immediately. Patience and persistence are greatly needed for any seeking soul. You may not be ready for the answer, which is why I do not give it straight away. You need further preparation, so gently, lovingly I go on preparing you until you are ready to receive the answer. When you are in a raised state, I reveal it to you from within.

You are living in the new where no books of knowledge have been written, where there is no pattern to follow. There is nothing hard and fast or cut and dried about this life. You cannot tell from one day to the next what is going to happen. This is the most thrilling and exciting time; whole new vistas keep opening up. The unkown is becoming known.

You no longer fear the unexpected. Often in the past fear has held you back from entering new realms and having new experiences. How much easier is it for Me to work My wonders when all resistance has gone and you are absolutely free at any time.

Become attuned to Me at all times and in all places. Find the perfect Oneness with Me. Any moment of the day or night you can do this instantly. Be at one with Me at all times. Become aware of Me consciously, raising your consciousness until we are One. You have to do something, take some action in order to bring this about. It doesn't just happen automatically.

Everything you do, do with purest Love. Do it for Me, for My sake, and Love will vibrate from it and will bring joy, happiness, peace of heart and contentment. Remember this at all times.

FREEDOM OF THE SPIRIT

7.   There is always something new to learn in this life. Keep open and ready to receive the new. Be flexible at all times. Let My spirit move you in the moment. Call it "Freedom of the Spirit".

When you are living by the Spirit, life is full of excitement. It is ever moving, filled with joy and the unexpected. How can you ever become bored or dull when you are living in this way? Life becomes dull and lifeless when you get into a fixed form and refuse to move out of it. Watch for this.

There are times in life when strict discipline is necessary. Every soul has to go through these times in the process of reaching Me. It is right to have a fixed time of quiet and meditation, of seeking and finding Me, of being still and listening to My still, small voice. Every child should learn discipline at an early age, when it is so much easier to learn and accept it. So, in this spiritual life, it is easier for a soul to learn discipline at the beginning; then it does not waste time kicking against the pricks, causing itself unnecessary pain and suffering.

Once a soul has learned the two vital lessons of discipline and obedience, it can truly live by the Spirit. I know that at any time of the day or night I can call upon that soul and that instantly that soul will be attuned to Me, ready to listen and obey My slightest whisper with instant obedience, with never a moment wasted by "wait a minute". This is a stage to be reached along the spiritual path.

If the desire is great enough and deep enough, nothing can stand in the way of achievement. Let nothing you do be half-hearted. Give all and you will indeed receive all. Lift up your heart and give Me constant thanks for all My good and perfect gifts.

LIVE FULLY IN THE MOMENT

8.   Stop striving, and live fully in the moment, finding perfect peace and stillness in that moment. Strain comes when you try to look too far ahead. All these things I have said many times, but you forget until you are once again brought to a standstill and realise that you are making the old mistakes again. They may seem to be small mistakes but they are vital ones and the sooner they are overcome, the better, for I need to use you all the time, which is not easy to do when there is stress or strain. Relax in My love and live fully in the moment.

Know that all is very well. Go on from there free, unburdened and unhampered by anything of the lower self. Every day is new, every day you are pioneering new paths and new realms. That is why you need Me as your constant guide and companion. Never travel this journey alone; keep ever aware of Me no matter what you are doing.

It is good, every now and then, to stop and realise that you are indeed pioneers and explorers into the New and that the way now opening up will be used by thousands and not just the few. It is easy to lose sight of the goal in everyday living and to fail to see how important it is. When you are too close to something or somebody, this can happen all too easily.

View those who are close to you from a distance; get your perspective right and in focus. When you have done that, forge ahead with new zest and joy in living. Realise how blessed you are to be where you are, living the life you live, being completely guided by Me. This is the way all must live who are moving into the new.

Blaze the trail with new enthusiasm. It is a glorious life and all are mightily blessed.

RISE TO GREAT HEIGHTS

9.   Rise, rise quickly into the realms of Light, of Truth, of Beauty, leaving all else behind! In an instant you can do this. The choice is always yours. When you feel low, depressed or weary, immediately do something about it. As you think, so you are. Remain in complete control of these thoughts and act swiftly.

When your thoughts become negative and you find yourself thinking unloving or critical thoughts towards another soul, change those thoughts and do it quickly. As you build up loving, positive thoughts towards every soul you come into contact with, you not only help those souls but help yourself as well and find yourself in those glorious higher realms where all is beauty. Watch your thoughts; never allow them to bind or hold you down.

I have so much to reveal to you and you must be free, free from all that would fetter you. Negative thoughts are like weights that hold you down.

You can control your whole outlook on life and your circumstances by your right thinking. This is a responsibility. When I say to you: "Rise, My child," you know exactly what to do—raise your thinking, and as you do so, you will rise to great heights.

Let your heart expand all the time. Love is needed everywhere. Remember that Love is service, Love is action, Love is not some woolly, vague emotion to be talked about. Learn to demonstrate it in all you do.

MAKE TIME

10.   There are many souls with hands outstretched seeking help and sustainment. Be ready to give help when asked and never turn a seeking, searching

soul away empty-handed. Give and give unstintingly. Never allow anything to be too much trouble. There is time for everything that is really necessary.

Make time by waking early in the morning when all is at peace and quietness envelops everything. Use that time to the full. Never regret spending precious time with Me. It is during that time that you grow spiritually, that you blossom and flower.

Times of self-discipline are good, are proof that your choice is to put Me and your service to Me first.

Put first things first. This choice is made the first moment you waken from sleep. Do you choose to indulge the self in further sleep? Are you willing to seek Me first?

Always you have to choose. Each day the choice lies before you anew; it is not something you do once which then becomes permanent. During the day— and every day—this choice lies in your hands.

In every decision you make, choose whether you make it for the self or whether you seek My divine guidance and follow that. Keep constantly on your toes; it is easy to slip and take the easy path, the self-indulgent one, and fail to do My will. Walk in My ways and do My will.

Let Me show you My wonders and glories.

THE KEY

11.   The key to all true, lasting happiness is to love Me with all your heart, with all your soul and all your mind and to love your neighbour as yourself. When this comes first and foremost, life becomes rich and wonderful. You can really say that life is indeed worth living.

See good in all things and in all people, be it just the tiniest spark. It can be fanned until it becomes a powerful flame and all that is discordant and disharmonious disappears into that flame and is consumed until only the purest gold is left.

Every soul seeks for happiness but often in the wrong way and in the wrong places and wonders why it cannot be found. See Me first and find Me; that is the simple answer. Put first things first, no matter what the cost or sacrifice. No sacrifice is too great to reach that goal.

It is vitally important that you have complete faith in what you are doing, that there is never a shadow of doubt. Be open and willing to accept anything, no matter how seemingly strange or fantastic. In the new anything can happen— and I mean anything. Never push something away because it does not fit into a well-worn or fixed form; accept it whether it is a thought or an experience.

Try to put it into words, no matter how seemingly inadequate, and give it form. The further into the new you go, the more of the old must be cast off, until eventually there is nothing of the old.

The old cannot exist in the new.

RESISTANCE CAUSES SUFFERING

12. Because you have suffered in this process, it does not mean that every soul has to suffer. It is resistance which causes suffering.

The new is unconventional and that goes against the grain with many. Man finds it hard to understand or even believe that I would ask anyone to do anything which does not fit into a nice, neat, conventional pattern.

I tell you that *all* fixed patterns are to be cast aside. I need you free and ready to do anything at any time;

Listen to My voice and obey.

When you do this, all is well and My wonders can be brought about.

I AM WITH YOU

13. Put on the whole armour of love. Stand firm and steadfast in My love. Allow nothing to disturb or distress you.

I am with you, therefore who can be against you?

Have I not told you that tests are good for you? They strengthen every fibre of your being, strengthen your faith and belief in Me and in My word.

The greater the test, the greater the strength.

Resent and resist nothing. Resist not evil. Overcome evil with good. Never hit back. When I say, "Turn the other cheek," I mean just that. Seek constantly that inner peace and stillness which nothing can touch or disturb. Work always from the centre outwards.

These are vital lessons which are being learnt at this time. Learn them swiftly. Lift up your heart in joy and thankfulness that you are being tested in this way. Become unshakable and rocklike.

Your foundations are in Me, therefore nothing can rock them or touch them.

A TIME OF REVELATION

14. I tell you that these are wonderful days, glorious days. Many truths are being revealed which have lain hidden. Accept all with a glad heart and sing for joy.

Together we explore these realms of great Light where truths have been hidden, to be revealed at this specific time.

This is a day of awakening, of revelations. The doors of heaven are swung wide open. Enter and carry down My gifts upon this earth. For those who have eyes to see, let them see. For those who have ears to hear, let them hear. For those who know Me and speak My word, let them do so fearlessly and joyously.

My wonders are brought down upon this earth.

The still, deep peace which is Mine enfolds you. Do My will.

LEARN TO BE

15.   Be at peace. Striving gets you nowhere; it simply leaves you exhausted and frustrated because you never seem to be nearer the goal. Just learn to be. When you have ceased striving, creep into My loving arms like a weary child. Encircled in those arms, feel the peace, comfort and complete Oneness with Me; feel yourself melt into Me.

It is all so simple, so natural, but its very simplicity prevents man from doing it. He is forever trying to complicate matters, making Me so inaccessible that it is impossible to reach Me direct. He thinks he has to do so by devious routes, great suffering and striving. How utterly foolish! What a complete waste of precious time and effort! I am within each one of you. Recognise this constantly; accept the simplicity of it. Walk and talk with Me at all times and in all places.

I am here to lift all burdens, to give answers to problems so that you become free to do My work. How can you do My work when you are tied up with yourself and your problems and feel weighed down? You must be free to rise, to move freely in those higher dimensions, to feel at one with Me, to function in Me, through Me and with Me.

You need no intermediary once you have accepted this Truth. I AM THAT I AM. I am within you and direct your whole life.

Live fully in the Now. Leave the past behind. Know that all is very well. Let Me use you more and more.

Allow nothing of the lower self to stand in the way.

UNDERSTANDING

16.   Keep your hand outstretched so that those in need may grasp it and be helped over the difficult places in life. When you have crossed those places of difficulty and are standing on the other side, you can be of help to those on the same path.

The pioneer always has the hardest task. Once he is over the chasm or has surmounted that difficult climb he makes it easier for those who are following behind. If he holds out his hand to help his fellowmen across, he can start them on the next part of their journey.

How necessary is deep understanding and sensitivity! Tread softly, yet with confidence. Be sure you know where you are going and why you are going there. Let there be a purpose and a plan running through all you do and all you say. Let there be no waste of words. Words have great power; use them wisely and guidedly. Have faith and confidence when you hold out a hand to a soul in need. You will help that soul — not in your own strength but in Mine. Do all with Me.

There is a great work to be done with so many souls in need. You will not fail them. Keep close to Me. Some will jump that chasm simply by holding your hand, another will need a rope, others will need a bridge. Great patience and understanding are needed. Encourage, yes, but never at any time force a soul to take a step it is not quite ready for.

Your radar must be kept in full working order all the time—never switch it off. Be at peace.

DIVINE ECONOMY

17.   I want to make it absolutely clear how vitally important it is when you raise your consciousness and rise to great heights and walk in those higher realms, that what you experience in those realms is brought down and recorded. I tell you that it does not matter how inadequately it is done, the fact that you do it is helping to bring down My heaven upon earth.

First of all it teaches you discipline which is always good, for every soul needs discipline. What I have to say can and will help others in the days to come as we are moving into the new.

So often what I have to say could be for so many, many souls on the same path. It is what can be called divine economy. The lessons you have learnt and are learning all the time along this spiritual path are to be passed on to others and greatly used.

I never ask you to do anything which is not absolutely necessary to your growth and the growth of others.

Cease questioning. Simply do My will with joy in your heart and be everlastingly grateful that I can use you in this way.

POSITIVE THINKING

18.   Life is so simple, yet so often you make it so difficult and complicated for yourself and for others by your wrong thinking. You stray away from the Truth, then wonder what is wrong and why all around you has become dull and difficult.

By changing your thinking from negative, life can change to a full and glorious life where you feel completely at one with Me and so at one with your fellow men. Your heart opens up and you find Love flowing through you where hitherto there was nothing. You become interested in those around you. You begin to feel their need. You turn more and more to Me to seek the answer. You feel part of a whole, never alone or isolated.

When life becomes too much for you and you want to run away from it all—stop. Be very still and seek within your heart. Think on these things, then do something about it.

Life is what you make it. I tell you it is a glorious life, a life filled with joy, with true happiness, with action.

You will find, as you accept it, that you are one with Me.

Seek My will and obey it. Peace be with you.

LAY ALL IN MY HANDS

19.   I say to you and I say to all, be very patient, persevere and be persistent—for only in this way can the goal be reached.

Look within your hearts, seek diligently and you will be shown what is the goal for you.

When your eyes have been opened, forge ahead and allow nothing to stand in your way. You will find that many things will try to stand in your way. This is where persistence is so necessary. Never vacillate.

You must know where you are going; otherwise you will become completely lost. There will be many things which will tempt you off the path, which will even pull you off it if you are not really strong and steadfast. Sweep aside difficulties because you are determined to get there come what may.

Keep close to Me. Never try to do what has to be done on your own. Let not your heart be heavy, for all is very well.

Lay all in My hands. Follow in My footsteps.

REALISATION

20.   Every soul along the spiritual path comes to a time when he is stripped of everything and stands before Me naked and in true humility.

When that time comes, he finds that it is the end, for he has nothing. Yet it is when he has reached that point of complete nothingness that he becomes everything. That is when he finds Me, the Lord his God.

He realises that without Me he is as nothing but with Me he is everything and nothing is impossible.

That is the turning point in his life. It may be a hard uphill struggle but never will he want to look back or choose the easy path. He may falter and stumble along the road, it may seem rough and rugged and at certain junctures the way may appear insurmountable.

He never gives up once his feet have been firmly planted on the path. He knows that he is no longer alone, that he can always seek Me and find Me. Together we will face the seemingly insurmountable and reach the heights. I am his ever present help. All he has to do is to ask. He is never refused help by Me.

The more he turns to Me, finds Me, does everything with Me, the more aware he becomes of our Oneness.

I never separate Myself from him.

MY LOVE IS LIMITLESS

21.   The very simplicity of this relationship with Me seems to be a stumbling block.

Why, My child? Because mankind does not know the true meaning of Love. When he does, he will never cut himself off from Me again.

My love is limitless. Nothing stops the flow of My love except the little self which is free to choose its own way. It turns its back on My love and demands its independence and so cuts itself off.

When man chooses to go My way, to walk in My footsteps, the floodgates are released. Once again he can become aware of the wonder of My love.

All this you know. You have suffered the pain and the ecstasy. Help others along the path so that they do not fall into the same pitfalls and so waste precious time. Make the way smooth.

Learn to be a wayshower. Turn them to Me.

KNOW MY JOY

22.   Be still and know Me, the Lord your God.

That is all you have to do—no stress nor striving.

I am there. You can only find Me when you still your whole being and find that peace which passes understanding. When your life is in turmoil and the mirror of your soul is rough, you fail to see the pure reflection within.

When you become very still, look within. The soul is like a still, clear pool and the reflection within that pool is perfect. Now, in that perfect stillness, find Me and know Me.

Open your heart. Accept all My good and perfect gifts. Give thanks for them. It is only a closed heart which is incapable of receiving. Throw open the portals wide and all is yours.

Joy, joy, joy—know My joy. Feel it surging within you until it bursts forth like the song of the lark as it soars upwards in sheer joy and delight and thanksgiving.

Your life is hid in Me and all is very well.

MY WILL IS BEING DONE

23.   As you become still, all chaos and confusion disappear and peace and harmony reign. Hold before you the perfect in everything and bring it about.

The wheels are turning. They may appear to be turning slowly, for it takes time for them to gain momentum. The whole situation and the future are assured. Even though you behold nothing at present, great strides have been made.

I tell you that this is to give comfort and reassurance during a period of drought and seeming inactivity. Force nothing; simply know that all is working out and only the perfect will transpire.

It is a strange time. Be still. Let every thought and action be guided by Me. My will is being done.

HOLD THIS IDEAL

24.   You are like a piece of blotting paper. You are absorbing Truth all the time. It is becoming a part of you. You are beginning to live and move and have your being in Truth.

I AM THAT I AM. I AM within you. I AM everywhere. I AM good. I AM Love.

Therefore, all is good, all is love, all is perfection. There is no imperfection anywhere around you. Let all this sink deep within you. Breathe it, know it, live it.

This is something you learn to live, to put into motion in your everyday living. The higher part of you knows these truths and it is the higher part you have to live by more and more. You can then say that your life is hid in Me, that you function from the I AM, from Me.

You are made in My image and likeness. You are perfect, even as I am perfect. You have created any imperfection by your lower mind. Give it no life. Let it die.

Become more and more conscious of this perfection everywhere. Erase from your thinking anything that is not perfect. Hold this ideal.

You will feel a new love for your fellow man. You will see the world as I made it—perfect.

Stretch until your consciousness, your awareness, holds nothing but the perfect. You are to do this until it is so.

WALK IN MY WAYS

25.   When you are doing something with My authority, never look back. Do it joyously; do it in the freedom of My spirit.

Hold these visions before you. See My wonders and My miracles come about and glorify Me.

See only My spirit before you; feel only My spirit within you.

Do My will and walk in My ways.

Let the light of My countenance shine and fill you with My truth.

Let not your heart be troubled. I am with you always.

I AM THE ARTIST

26.   Come to Me each day like an empty cup ready to be refilled.

Each day is new. Rid yourself of those petty annoyances and irritations, of all that would mar the perfection of today.

The canvas is clean. Let the picture commence and know that it will be perfect.

I am the Artist. Know only perfection and create only perfection.

Learn to do this each day.

The more you are aware of Me in your everyday living, the higher you rise into those new realms.

DO ALL WITH ME

27.   You will have wonderful surges forward. Then there must be a time of consolidating before the next forward surge.

Accept this as part of the process and never become downhearted.

You cannot remain on the mountain top all the time.

Contrast is good for you. Never go back but always a little forward.

This is a time of rejoicing. Expect the best and bring it about.

See Me in everything, in everyone. Let your awareness of Me be acute, your love for Me growing day by day.

I tell you that tremendous things are happening at this time. Nothing is static. Do all with Me.

SIT AND BE

28.   Still the whole of your being. Sit and BE.

Listen to the birds singing My praises, lifting up their hearts in sheer joy and delight. In their song of praise feel Me and know Me.

I am everywhere. I am in everything. I am within that stillness within your soul.

You can find Me at all times, for I am here, closer than breathing, nearer than hands and feet. Become ever conscious of Me and of My presence.

You breathe all the time, for breathing is life, yet you are seldom aware of your breathing unless you think about it, perhaps trying to control if for a special purpose. Then you are aware that you are alive and kept alive because of your breathing. You know that if you stopped breathing, life would no longer flow through you. All this you take for granted most of the time.

So it is with Me, with My presence. It is always there. Like breathing, you take Me for granted and forget My very existence. This is what the majority of mankind does. They are completely unaware of Me.

You know the wonder of being at one with Me. Keep this awareness of Me ever before you. Never allow it to fade.

BRING ME INTO EVERYTHING

29.   Learn to bring Me into everything.

No matter what you are doing, be aware of My presence.

When you are aware, you will want to do everything to My honour and glory. When you find yourself doing something half-heartedly or with lack of enthusiasm, you can be sure you are doing it without being aware of Me.

If you are down on your knees scrubbing a floor, you can do it with Me. If you have soapsuds up to your elbows, you can do it with Me. But whether you are aware of Me or not is up to you.

Be ever conscious of Me.

Many souls refuse to accept this intimacy with Me and see Me standing afar off.

Seek and ye shall find.

ALL ARE MY PERFECT CREATION

30. All is perfect, for all comes from Me, the Creator of all things.

I can only create the perfect. I do not know imperfection, for imperfection is unreality. Perfection is reality.

Raise your consciousness until you see imperfections vanish like mist in the rays of the sun, until there is nothing left in you and around you but My perfection.

When you stop and consider what is meant by that word "perfection", you see only harmony, peace, beauty, love, all around you.

Your heart opens like a glorious flower and you see all men in My image and likeness.

You cannot dislike anyone, you cannot be annoyed and irritated at anyone, because all are My children, all are My perfect creation.

Think of those words: "As you think, so you are."

Know that as you become aware that man is created in My image and likeness and that I am perfect, you will become aware that all mankind is perfect.

LIVE REALITY

31. As you raise your consciousness above personalities, you rise into that new dimension where all is one with Me and you can only see the perfect.

Try it the next time you are out of harmony with a soul. Raise your consciousness and see only My perfect creation in that soul. As you do this, a great sense of peace and harmony will descend upon you.

This is all very practical. Live it. Practise it. See that it really does work.

When you see how wonderfully it works, you will realise that it springs from Me.

My ways are perfect. Walk in My ways. Live reality.

YOUR ROCK-LIKE FOUNDATION

32.   Be like the wise man who built his house upon a rock. When the rain descended and the floods came, the winds blew and beat upon the house, nothing moved because it was founded upon a rock.

These are not easy times, these times of not really knowing what is happening. You can so easily be thrown off course if your faith is not strong and grounded in Me. That is your rock-like foundation.

Become still in the midst of chaos and confusion. Know Me and know that no matter what seems to be happening around you, out of all chaos and confusion only the perfect can come about. This is vitally important at this time.

Be still. Watch My wonders. Glorify Me. See My hand in everything.

Resist not evil but overcome evil with good.

BE CONSCIOUS OF ME

33.   Be conscious of our closeness. Be still and listen. If you are constantly busy rushing around, you forget to listen, and then wonder why things do not go smoothly and why you are not at peace.

Seek ye first My kingdom and My righteousness. When you have done that, everything else will fit into place and run smoothly.

No matter how busy you are, put Me first in everything. Remember this and see how smoothly everything else will run.

Time spent the first thing in the morning with Me means more than at any other time. In this time you become attuned to Me, then during the busy day you can bring Me into everything you are doing and thus bring peace and harmony where but a few moments ago were chaos and confusion.

Keep doing this all the time. Put Me first in everything. See how different life becomes.

THE INDIVIDUAL CONTRIBUTION

34.   Be as simple and as natural as a little child. Never try to be anything else. Each soul has something unique to contribute to the whole and the whole would not be complete without that contribution. It is resistance which causes strain and stress.

You are moving all the time into a new age, leaving the old behind forever. See before you the great Light and move towards it constantly. Let it draw you like a magnet. Walk into it with a full and joyous heart. Be prepared to take any action asked of you without any feeling of trepidation. Be absolutely fearless.

Can you feel it seeping in until you are becoming Light?

You talk blightly about 'building a Light body', of being able to translate your body by raising your vibrations so much that you become invisible. This is something each individual has to bring about by his thinking, his longing, his desire to do so. There is no better time than now.

Draw forth the thought of relaxing into Light and become that Light. New and wonderful things are waiting to be recognized.

Recognition is the first step and the knowledge that with Me all things are possible. *Know* this as a *Fact*.

I infil you with My Light until you become purest Light.

THERE IS THE PERFECT ANSWER

35. Never allow any trace of sadness to enter your life. These are joyous wonderful days, so much is going forward on every plane.

Never become afraid of the tremendous power which is being released at this time. Simply understand that it has to be harnessed and channelled so that it can be used to the full. This power must not be allowed to get out of hand or be dissipated. I can assure you that it is in very capable hands.

There is the perfect answer to every problem; therefore, take time and seek for it until you find it. It is not always the big things that cause disorder; often it is the small things.

Be sensitive, loving, guided. Never waste energy unnecessarily. There is much to be done but let every action be guided and have My full blessing.

THE ONE VOICE

36. An animal knows its master's voice amongst many voices and obeys it. It listens for that voice and ignores all others. When training begins, it will rush from one voice to another, pulled around from pillar to post, completely muddled and confused. As training continues, that one voice becomes clearer, more distinct than all the others. That voice becomes greatly loved and no other matters.

So it has been with your training. There have been severe tests and trials but the training has been invaluable. You now know My voice, No matter what is happening around you, and that is all that matters.

GREATER WORKS SHALL YE DO

37.   Take heed of those words you have read so many times: "The works that I do shall ye do also and greater works shall ye do." The promise was not that you should do the same, but even greater. You read these words but it takes long for you to realise that they were given to you. *You* have to accept them as part of your life and do something about them. You have to give them life force. You have to become My hands and feet.

It is good to stop and consider the Christ ministry, the Christ consciousness. It is good to realise that this is within you when you are consciously aware of it and when you are willing to take the responsibility it entails. You must not only be willing, you must know that you can go forth and in your daily living do even greater works, work even greater miracles. You must know this without a shadow of doubt.

Be not afraid of these words. They are the truth. They have been spoken *to you.* What are you going to do about them; just read and re-read them and leave them for somebody else to do something about, or are you going to make them a part of your living? It is up to you. All My promises are living promises, but you have to make them live. Consider deeply what I am saying to you.

Find peace and contentment in doing My will, in seeing it manifest in form all around you.

WORK BY THE SPIRIT

38.   Because the ego does not always behold what is going on, this does not mean that nothing is going on. Let your heart feel, let your consciousness expand, be aware of the wonderful transformation now taking place.

All the vibrations are being stepped up. You feel this strongly when you are in a raised state. Never strain to understand the things of the Spirit. By becoming still, you will see the reflection and you will understand. You cannot expect to fathom My mysteries with the mind; what is happening is of the Spirit and has to be understood on the level of the Spirit.

Work by the Spirit and from the Spirit, with the Spirit within the very centre of your being. Live, move and understand in the spirit of truth and righteousness. Feel the freedom of the Spirit and rise on wings of Love and Light into those realms with a heart full of praise and thanksgiving, feeling My Peace and Love within you.

The Way is now open. Walk thou in it and do My will.

BECOME AS A ROCK

39. Let your faith be strong and unshakable. Be glad and rejoice when your faith is put to the test, for this strengthens it until it becomes as a rock, able to withstand the storms and tempests of life without being shaken in any way. It is vital to stand firm, to know the truth and to stand by it.

Silence is strong, whereas words can weaken and cause chaos. So be still and seek Me in the silence. Feel My power and strength and in this way you can help.

Let not your heart be troubled over anything. Radiate love, asking nothing in return. Listen and obey. This is the way to find peace, happiness and harmony.

Change your thinking and you change your whole outlook. Believe My words, treasure them and above all *live them*. Your blessings are as numerous as the stars in heaven. Recognise this and accept it joyfully.

THE CHRYSALIS

40. Think of a butterfly emerging from the comfort and security of its chrysalis. Suppose the butterfly stopped in its process of emerging and said,"No, I cannot leave this place. I don't know what may lie outside." Suppose it stopped and refused to move out. What would happen? It would be failing in its own evolution, and if it remained in its chrysalis, it would simply shrivel up and die.

So it is with you, My child. To refuse to move on because you are afraid of the unknown would most certainly hold up your evolution.

I have the most wonderful surprises and joys awaiting you as you step forth fearlessly into this new adventure, as you *emerge* from your chrysalis. There is nothing to fear. Only the perfect will result from this advance on your part, a whole new opening up of many untold mysteries and wonders.

Remember, My chold, I AM with you always, no matter where you are or what you are doing. I AM there guiding and guarding you.

ACCEPT THE FACT

41. Accept the fact that tremendous things are happening on the inner which will shortly manifest on the outer, changes which will affect every man, woman and child on this earth and will also affect the whole universe. Have absolutley no fear, no matter what happens.

Find the centre of peace and stillness within your consciousness and there remain, completely protected, absolutely secure. For I AM there in the midst of you. You shall become like a stronghold, like a fortress of light. Many souls will be drawn to your side; spread your wings over them as a mother hen does to protect her chicks and give them security and warmth.

Again I remind you, turn no one away from your door. Give them love and warmth. Make them feel welcome, wanted, a needed part of the whole. Turn no man away empty; share with all My divine gifts. All I have is yours; therefore, give freely, as all has been given freely to you. Count not the cost and count not the loss, for all will be returned a thousandfold. Keep your heart open wide and let My divine love flow through you. Watch and pray. Listen to My voice so that you miss nothing and find the true joy in living and moving and having your being in Me.

BEHOLD MY WONDERS COMING ABOUT

42.   Time means less and less. It is hard to believe that the season is changing, that the summer has passed, that so much has happened in so short a time, and yet this is but the beginning of a mighty speeding up, of mighty changes, not just for individuals but for the whole of this earth.

Learn to let go. Remember this in the days to come, for it is important. Have no fixed pattern or plans. Be flexible. Let go completely at times and relax.

Look back at this past year. See clearly the mistakes you have made and how you can rectify them. Learn to share work. Allocate it. Never feel that you ought to do something because *you* can do it more quickly. It is right for others to add their vibrations, for them to feel a part of the whole, to accept responsibility and to grow in the process. Never be possessive, even of a job— share everything. Everything should be done with love for Me and for each other.

There are important lessons to be learnt and learnt quickly. Never wallow in past mistakes. See them clearly for what they are and do something about them *now*.

Behold My wonders coming about.

LIFE IS LIKE A TREASURE HUNT

43.   Life is like a treasure hunt; one clue leads to the next. First find the clue and set about deciphering it. This may take time, patience and

perseverance, but until it has been deciphered and understood you cannot go on to the next clue. It is necessary to be still and at peace in order to work out where you are going and what you are going to do.

You cannot go through life rushing from one activity to another. You need time to consolidate your position and to be at peace.

You will find that there are not many souls who really desire peace and stillness. They say that they do, but when they are alone with nothing to distract them, they are lost and do not know what to do with themselves. The very stillness and quietness frightens them.

Is it any wonder that the world is in such a turmoil? Man refuses to take time to know his true self, to delve deep within, but only if he does this can he reach the heights.

Every moment spent in peace and solitude, in communion with Me, brings you nearer to the truth and opens up a new world, the world of Spirit.

Live fully in the moment, taking time to be with Me. Together let us decipher the next clue and discover the greatest secret of the universe: that we are One.

WHEN THERE IS CONFLICT

44. When there is conflict or a closed mind, it is impossible to be a pure channel for My divine inspiration. That is why it is necessary to become still within, no matter how active you may be outwardly, for in that stillness you become aware of Me. Your mind is no longer closed and I can work in you and through you.

This year of earth is a very special year. The jigsaw puzzle will suddenly fall into place, one piece after another will find its rightful place — and the glory of what is to come will astound you all. Accept it all and take your specific place in the pattern of the whole. The less the resistance, the greater the joy. All is One with Me.

A HELPING HAND

45. Each day stretch out a helping hand to those in need of help and understanding. Keep your heart wide open so that My Love can flow forth and answer the need in hungry hearts. Listen patiently to all who come.

Let Me guide your every word of advice; then you can only help that soul and not hinder by wrong advice. Say nothing rather than the wrong thing. When you are in doubt, be still. In that stillness doubts will vanish and you will know the right answer. Give it with confidence and authority, knowing that it is My authority. It does not matter whether the advice is approved of or not; you are not pandering to the little self, you are reaching up to the higher self in that soul and the higher part will recognise and accept it.

It is vitally important that you do all from the highest motives. You hold a great responsibility; therefore, let Me guide your every step. Accept today as a very special day and give, give give.

LIVE MY WORD

46.   A small child can be sitting in a room which is chaotic, with friction all around him, yet, if he is playing with a precious toy or is engrossed in a game, he can be blissfully unaware of anything discordant. He is concentrating on that one thing. So it is with you, My child. When there is discord and confusion around you, keep your heart and mind stayed on Me. Turn within and find that peace and stillness which nothing can touch or disturb.

More and more you will find the need to turn to that centre within. When you walk into a room and there is obviously discord, do not allow yourself to become part of it. Rise above it and become consciously aware of Me, that I AM there within you, that I AM peace and love and harmony, that I AM truth and understanding.

Put this advice into practice on all occasions. You will be given many opportunities; therefore, do not forget. You have something constructive to contribute, never hesitate to put it into action. Words without action are as nothing.

Live My word.

GROW IN STATURE

47.   You must grow in stature. There are times when you can only do this alone, with no one to lean upon or support you.

If you go through life with a constant prop, how can you expect to become strong and steadfast so that others in need may lean against you and draw from you?

Learn quickly, My child. Time is moving fast and everything is speeded up tremendously. There is no time to be lost. Do what has to be done, then move ahead to the next step joyously, with praise and thanksgiving, and with deep stillness and peace in your heart.

ADVANCE MY PLAN ON EARTH

48.   Every time you stop and become consciously aware of Me and listen to that still, small voice, you are helping to advance My plan on earth. You are in tune, in rhythm with the things that really matter in life. I am able to use you because in that state of awareness you become My hands and feet. Life has a purpose. It becomes a joy and a pleasure; nothing is humdrum, dull or boring.

You can be in this state of awareness every second of every day. Just think of it:—you need never be out of harmony with your surroundings or with those you contact when your mind is stayed on Me.

I AM always there, but you have free choice whether you wish to be consciously aware of Me or not. It is simply up to you.

WITHIN YOUR BEING

49.   Arise, put on the whole armour of God and reflect that love in the whole of your living. Look not for love without; find it within and then reflect it out.

Within your being you hold Me, the Lord your God.

This is a staggering thought. Stop for a moment and consider it.

You have life within you and I AM Life. You have love within you and I AM Love. You have Spirit within you and I AM Spirit. ALL is within you—you as an individual.

Therefore, I AM within every individual. Therefore, you are one with Me and one with your fellowmen, because I AM within every living soul and all souls are living.

As you think on these lines, you become closer and closer to your fellowmen and closer and closer to Me. You realise that there is no division, no separation. As you realise this, you feel a great joy well up within you and you become aware of Me and of My Presence. Dwell on these thoughts; they expand and raise your consciousness, bringing you, in a complete circle, to the realisation of My wonder and My perfection of your oneness with Me.

My child, eventually ALL will have to complete that circle, all will have to come back to the beginning, will have to find their relationship with Me, the Lord their God.

Unless you become as little children and are born again in Spirit and in Truth, you cannot enter into the kingdom of heaven. This is a very humbling thought—and this is why mankind, with all its knowledge, finds it so difficult.

THE NEW VIBRATIONS

50.   I speak of the speeding up of the situation and you wonder exactly what I mean. Then unexpectedly you feel what you describe as a 'universal speeding up of the vibrations'. It starts within, like a ripple of extreme excitement, and that ripple seems to go out and out into the whole universe. Nothing seems to stop it. Instead of the vibrations stopping, they become more and more powerful until you are tingling like something filled with electricty.

You will find many souls going through similar experiences. This is a heightening of the vibrations of all those who are responsive. These things could not happen to you unless you were willing and open to them. You have to be constantly aware of changes, aware that you are being used to bring down to this level what is happening in the higher realms.

This raising and heightening of vibrations is what must happen to all who are to pass through this earth's travail without being affected and becoming part of the chaos and confusion.

Let My peace and love surround and infil you. Glory in the new. All is truly wonderful—open your eyes and behold it.

BE AWARE OF MIRACLES

51.   Be aware of the miracles and wonders which are happening all around you all the time. It is so easy to busy yourself in the mundane things and to fail to see My wonders. Life is never dull; it is full to overflowing with the most thrilling things.

Gradually the lost sheep will all be gathered into the fold. Think often of the story of the prodigal son and give thanks for it, for this is a most glorious example of love and understanding.

BE APPROACHABLE

52.   How important it is that you be always approachable. When a soul is in need of help, it is in a sensitive state and tentatively puts out its feelers for help.

When you are close to Me, that soul will feel the understanding and love and immediately will be drawn to you and so receive the help it needs. Be ready and on the alert to give the helping hand.

Behold the *Limitlessness* of My love and glory in it. Peace be with you and with all those around you.

THINK BIG THOUGHTS

53. Think big thoughts, My child. Anything, absolutely anything, can happen now. Tremendous power has been released and nothing can stop its onrush. Arise and walk in the new.

What is happening now is a uniting of all the facets of the work you are doing for Me until all is one and there is no division.

I pour My blessings on each one of you. Feel that circle of love and peace surround you. Shout "Hallelujah and Glory Be," for all are risen! All are one.

ACCEPT THIS REALISATION

54. As you raise your consciousness and realise your Oneness with Me, there is no duality. Love flows through you in ever-increasing power and you see only the perfect and good in all.

How necessary it is for you to do this. *Really* understand that mankind is made in My image and likeness and is therefore perfect. If I AM *your* Father, I AM the Father-Mother-God of *all* mankind.

Accept this realisation.

BE FAITHFUL IN SERVICE

55. Be faithful in service. Doing something for the first time can be exciting and thrilling, doing it for the second and third time can be quite a thrill, but when you have to do something day in and day out, it takes risen thinking and risen consciousness to do it in the right spirit. You have to tackle it with new eyes each time, so do it to My honour.

TODAY IS A GLORIOUS DAY

56. Today is a glorious day. See beyond to what you know it can be— beautiful sunshine and warmth, the right weather for the garden for ripening fruit, the right weather for those on holiday, the right weather to bring real joy and happiness to all around you.

When you go into a shop, make a point of expressing your delight in something lovely. Your positive thought can lift the thoughts of all those you contact. Your attitude can help uplift and bring joy into everyone's life as you bring it into your own.

When you can do this all the time, you will have truly reached a turning point in your life. Remember, as long as you have Love in your heart, you are invulnerable, no harm can touch you. The fiery darts of the enemy cannot penetrate, for Love is your perfect armour.

Love is your protection, that divine Love which comes from Me. Open your heart and let it be filled to overflowing, then radiate it out all the time.

JUST CONSIDER

57.   Just consider that for years I have been talking to you, guiding you leading you into the paths of righteousness. Throughout the years, your faith and truth have become stronger. You trust My word implicitly. Come what may, now you know that My word is your guide and that your obedience to My word is the only thing that matters even if you have to stand completely alone.

Until a soul becomes aware of Me, of My word or My power and My love, that power and that love cannot become manifest in that soul, for it has no life force and so they do not become living vibrating words.

It is up to you to make My words a reality — so much rests in your hands and in the action you take.

TESTS ALL ALONG THE WAY

58.   Only as you are willing to keep your heart and mind open can you learn and expand. This is vitally important to your inner growth. If you become rigid and close your mind to some new concept, refusing to delve into it, you form a blockage which stops your advancement along this spiritual path.

There must be absolute frankness and freedom in every respect in order to enable you to expand. If you shut your mind and tell yourself that you know the answer, you immediately close a door which should be left open.

There are tests all along the way and these tests are strengthening, they should never weaken a soul. Seek and find the answer to every problem. Tests turn you more and more to Me, the source of all knowledge. Anything that turns you to Me is good. The more often you turn to Me the closer we become, the more aware you become of our Oneness.

Every day there is something new to learn. Be alert; do not miss it. It may be a very obvious lesson, at other times it may be subtle and so carefully camouflaged that you may fail to see it as a lesson and miss something important, so keep alert.

There are times when it is necessary to watch and pray, there are times when immediate action should be taken. When action is called for, let there be no hesitation, no procrastination, for then is the time to take action. As you do so, you will find a great peace and stillness which comes from obeying My voice.

KNOW WHAT YOU ARE DOING

59.   You must know what you are doing. You must know where you are going. This conscious awareness is vitally important to your advancement along the spiritual path—there is nothing vague about this. You may not know where the next step is going to take you, but nevertheless the next step has to be taken in complete faith and confidence and in the assurance that by taking it you will eventually reach the goal.

Do what has to be done in utter confidence, nothing wavering. Be not swayed by any outside influence. Seek the answer from within, find it and act upon it. Learn to act only from that withinness—this is where you will always find Me. Inner awareness, inner conviction, is all you need act upon.

When you place yourself in My hands to use as I will, you cannot hold a part of yourself back. I ask for all, for only in this way can I use My channel. There cannot be two parts of you, for we are one and you have to become aware of that oneness until you see the two melt into one and know fully the meaning of the words: "I and My Father are One; I am in Him and He is in me"—no longer any separateness.

This is a new life and this life is perfect. Walk in it in joy and confidence.

DWELL NOT ON THE PAST

60.   Dwell not on the past. Use it to illustrate a point, then leave it behind. Nothing really matters except what you do *now* in this instant of time. From this moment onward you can be an entirely different person, filled with love and understanding, ready with an outstretched hand, uplifted and positive in every thought and deed.

You know that I AM perfect; therefore, you are perfect. As you dwell on that perfection in every soul, you draw it forth. It may be hidden deep but it is there, and with patience and perseverance you cannot fail to find it. Go, seek for it—never be put off by the outer shell. Crack it open with love and understanding.

Behold My wonders within every soul, for they are there.

STAND BACK

61.   Stand back and admire My handiwork. Study every detail and see the perfection of it. It is necessary to stop and be still and absorb the wholeness of the world around you.

When you rush around being so busy all the time, you miss so much; life becomes a blur and the really important facts in life are missed.

The truth must be revealed in all its wonder and glory. Be not concerned regarding those who refuse to accept it. Many souls will be temporarily blinded by the light but gradually their eyes will become accustomed to it.

Feed My sheep with the food of the Spirit. Let My word go forth to satisfy all those who are hungry and ready. The great awakening has already begun.

BLESSED ARE THEY

62.   Blessed are they that thirst after truth and love, for then shall all things be added unto them.

When a soul is ready to shoulder the responsibility of wielding My divine powers, then shall those powers be his to use for My work. This can only be given when one is ready and there is nothing of the lower self to mar perfection. Those powers which have been released at this specific time have to be used only by those who are fully dedicated to My work so that only good can come forth.

You will find that many souls will now choose the way of Light. They will make their final decision to choose My way. Send forth this powerful ray which will do its strange work of dividing the wheat from the chaff, the sheep from the goats.

Perfect love casts out all fear. Be at peace in all you do and know that all is well and working according to My plan.

CLAIM YOUR HERITAGE

63.   Everything you do, do to My honour and glory. Let My light shine through it all, revealing nothing but the truth. Seek nothing for the self. Know Me and love Me with all your heart, mind and soul.

Let your love for Me infiltrate every atom of your whole being until you are all Light and Love.

Let your aims be high. Claim your rightful place in My kingdom. Claim your true heritage. Know that I AM within you. Let not a single doubt enter into you. Know this in truth for *now* you are My children.

You do not have to wait until you are perfect before you claim this heritage. Claim it now. This is the truth. Accept it.

REVELATION

64.   This is an historic and momentous time in the progress of man. At this time the veil is being rent in two and that which has been hidden through the ages is now to be revealed. The secrets of the sages will no longer be secrets, for all shall know about them.

The Book of Life has now been unlocked and the truths held within it are being brought into the open for all men to see and to use.

Revelation upon revelation is now being revealed. My glories are now being manifested here on earth. It is all happening *now*. Open your eyes and behold it. Miss nothing. All is there for all men to behold when they choose to open their eyes to do so.

The time is at hand when these words will become reality: "The Son of God will appear in full glory for all to see." Be ready, for no man knows the day nor the hour. Be prepared at any moment to receive Him. I tell you to be surprised at nothing.

THE WORDS I SPEAK

65.   The words I speak to you are precious beyond earthly treasures, for they are from everlasting to everlasting. They are Life, they are Love, they are Me — and I AM Life and I AM Love.

You cannot say that you love Me and in the next breath say that you dislike one single soul. Expand your consciousness until you begin really to understand that all mankind is made in My image and likeness — all — not the selected few.

See the best in every soul. Seeing draws it out and enables others to see it in themselves. So the God-man is drawn out and developed in every soul.

SEE NO LIMITATION

66.   Stretch, My child, in every direction. Let your heart, your consciousness expand, and see no limitations. All the time there are important lessons

to learn quietly and unobtrusively. Be there when needed; blend quickly into the background when the need has been met. Step out of your routine, out of your well-worn rut, and move all the time into the new. Live entirely in the spirit.

My peace I give. Accept it. Never push it aside. Let it sink into you, around you. Radiate it. The more hectic life becomes, the greater the need for that inner peace and stability.

See that clear, still pool within you. Only when it is like a mirror can you reflect My Love and Light without blemish.

WORK IN UNISON

67.   Each one of you has a part to play in the days ahead. Each part is unique and entirely different, but each part makes up the perfect whole. Contribute your part at the right time and in the right place.

Like a play being enacted, each player has his or her part. All the players are not on the stage at the same time except at the end. Some of the parts are leading parts, some are small ones; nevertheless everyone is needed to produce the perfect play.

Work in unison, entering and doing your part, then withdrawing into the background to watch and learn while the others take their parts. In this there is perfect rhythm.

CONSIDER A MOMENT

68.   This morning I want you to dwell wholly on Me.

What am I? I AM Life and Life is eternal. I AM Love and Love is limitless. I AM Spirit and Spirit is everywhere.

Then consider a moment; I AM within you. Your body is My holy temple and I dwell within that temple. Is it any wonder that I ask you to expand your consciousness in order to make more room for Me?

I AM *your* consciousness. I cannot be limited, for I AM limitless. As you become ever more consciously aware of Me, you cannot help expanding to make more and more room for Me.

The world of spirit, that world within, grows daily. There is a steady growth, a steady expansion; there is less and less room for the old, for you are outgrowing the old to make room for the new.

Yes, My child, all this is going on. That is why, every now and then, you have growing pains. You feel so full of praise and thanksgiving that you want to burst all bonds, you want to sing and to weep. Sometimes these are tears of bewilderment because growth is being so speeded up.

Ponder on all this. Take time. Be still. Absorb it.

Let the wonder of it make your heart cry out in sheer joy and happiness and freedom—and above all deep, deep gratitude.

REJOICE AND BE OF GOOD CHEER

69.   Rejoice and be of good cheer, for the doors stand wide open. Enter and share the wonders of the new. Walk with a light tread. Dance like a piece of thistledown through My many mansions. Enjoy to the full everything that is happening. Expect only the best, the most beautiful and glorious—and behold, all things open up before you.

All *is* there for you to behold. Miss nothing. My finger is pointing the way and those of the light behold it and walk in My ways. Go with all that is happening.

Your heart is full—let it overflow. You saw a chalice of silver light overflowing, and the pouring forth of that liquid made smooth all things which it touched. That is My love flowing forth from hearts which have been split wide open, freeing the love to flow with ever-increasing power and strength.

The need is great. Never at any time stem the flow of that love; never be afraid to demonstrate it openly. What is the use of saying that you love someone if you are afraid to demonstrate that love on the outer? It becomes like empty words without power. Let go and let Me use you as I will, freely, joyously.

Rejoice and behold all things become *new.*

ADVANCE WITH JOY

70.   Open the door of your consciousness wide so that there is a firm flow of My divine inspiration in and out. As you do this, your understanding will grow and expand and the things of the spirit will develop. All I need is a receptive instrument so that My truths can be imparted. Put first things first. Find the right path, the way of the Spirit.

The way of the spirit you must tread with only Me as your companion and guide. You can take no human companions with you along this path; it is straight and narrow and there is no room. Alone we tread the path of the spirit.

It can be the most exciting and thrilling adventure you have ever experienced, for you are entering new realms, exploring new dimensions, and you never know what is going to happen next.

Be not faint-hearted. There are ever greater and more wonderful realms to be opened up, more and more and more. Advance with joy and praise. Allow nothing to stop your advancing along My spiritual path.

RISEN BEING

71.   As you talk about risen being, as your consciousness rises and expands in this thought, it becomes more and more a part of you. You begin to live it, to be it, and the longing in you to do this helps in many ways.

It is as if you were completely blind and could see no light—in fact you did not know the meaning of light—and *now* you have been made whole and can see for the first time. The things you see are so wonderful that you find it difficult to believe they are real—you keep stretching your consciousness to touch them. You handle them in your consciousness in wonderment and find that they are reality, that you can live and be in this risen state, not occasionally but all the time.

Never pull back or doubt this thought. It is fact; the more you dwell upon it, the more real it becomes.

You wonder why you have been so blind and unable to see this truth as fact until recently. My child, you were not ready. There is a right time for everything. Now is the time for the great awakening.

What each soul does with this falling away of the scales before its eyes is up to each individual. Some will glory in the revelations, some will try to draw the glory to the self, some will turn their backs in fear and disbelief and will walk straight back into their self-made darkness. This is now the dividing of the ways. You will see it happening all around you. Be surprised at nothing, for this time is a time of wonderment.

LET THE WORLD GO BY

72.   Be still. Let the world go by, but seek peace and stillness, which are absolutely essential.

Never be too tired to listen to My voice. Be aware of that still, small voice within you, guiding you, prompting you, giving you the right answer to every problem. This is what makes you tick! If you closed down this part of yourself, you would become like a clock that had not been wound up and had stopped ticking, or a piece of machinery that had been clogged by dirt and needed cleaning before it could work again.

Think on those things, My child. Realise just how vital is that contact you have with Me. Seek peace and stillness at all times.

How necessary it is to be faithful in service and to enjoy the service whatever it may be. Approach it every day with new eyes, realising how important and essential this is.

Start *now* doing that same routine job with an entirely new attitude. Stop and look at it from a new angle; stand back and look at it upside down if this will help you change your attitude towards it.

When a child does the washing up for the first time, it is the most thrilling thing it has ever done. The soap suds are fun, the water dripping off the cups and plates is a lovely spectacle, everything is a wonderful game and it dwells on every piece of china in sheer delight. How about every time you do the washing up? Stop and see it with the eyes of a child.

Nothing in life should be dull. Try this out today as an experiment and see what a difference it can make. Do it with the right attitude and enjoy everything you do. Life is what you make it. Make it a thing of sheer beauty and harmony.

ALL ARE MADE IN MY IMAGE

73. I have asked you constantly to expand your consciousness. There is no limit to that expansion. Grow slowly but surely as nature does. Open that single inner eye within you; see all that is perfect. See My wonders and glories all around you; see Me reflected in your fellowmen. Know that all are made in My image and likeness, that perfection is the real and all else illusion. Demonstrate what you feel within.

GO YOUR WAY DOING MY WILL

74. When a truth has been revealed to you from within, you understand that truth because it is a part of you. You know that you are standing on an unshakable foundation, and you can speak on it with absolute authority and confidence.

Remember that you are in the world but not of it; therefore, have no longing for the things of the world which are here today and gone tomorrow. Seek always the things of the spirit which are eternal, from everlasting to everlasting.

In quietness and confidence go your way, doing My will.

REMEMBER THAT I AM LIFE

75.   Keep on raising your consciousness and see beyond the immediate; see the real, the spiritual, the perfection of My creation. It is there in everything and everyone.

You will be severely tested from time to time, but as you peel off layer upon layer of disillusionment and unreality, you will find that perfect creation of Mine in its full beauty and glory.

You will find your whole life beginning to change. You will find yourself living in peace and harmony—because you are creating it for yourself by your right approach to life. Remember that I am life; therefore, it is your right to approach Me, the source of all, the creator of all that is perfect.

You can find a perfect freedom which protects you from all that would harm you. Stand firm in your belief that I am guiding your life.

NO IDLE WORDS

76.   Let there be no idle words spoken. There is power in words and that power must not be dissipated but channelled in the right direction.

Watch your tongue—remember that silence is golden!

I WANT YOU TO KNOW

77.   Be grateful for everything that helps you to expand your consciousness. Every step that makes you rise is a step in the right direction and should be welcomed. See these as stepping-stones and dance along them joyously and sure-footedly with the assurance that you cannot fail to reach the goal. Do this whole-heartedly.

This is an exciting life. Nothing is dull or uninteresting when done with raised consciousness. It may be the same old job you have done thousands of times, but now you are doing it from a different dimension and therefore it appears to be entirely different. It takes on a new purpose for you are doing *all* for Me.

See it like a dark room when someone walks into it and puts his hand on a switch and instantly all is light. This transformation can be just like that. There need be no twilight hour.

I want you to *know* that this can happen and you will find it happening to you now. You feel that this is a mighty leap from one stepping-stone to the next. So it is, but you have wings on your feet and you know that all things are possible, so you can take that leap in absolute confidence and know that you will land safely.

I never fail you nor forsake you, but am with you and within you to help you over every transition.

GOD SPOKE TO ME
Part Three

INTRODUCTION

Reflect My Light and Love like beacons in a darkened world.
Nothing shall remain hidden when you are ready and prepared for its
revelation. As the ground must be dug and prepared before the seeds can be
planted, so your understanding and consciousness have to be prepared, raised
and expanded before you are ready to receive My truths which have been
hidden through the ages but which are *now* to be revealed to mankind as it
moves into the New Age.

This will cause upheavals in many lives. It will not be comfortable, for there is
bound to be chaos and confusion while the sifting and sorting take place.
Those who expected to move into the New Age with ease will find that this is
not the case. You can help speed things up by going with it and not causing
resistance, just as birth is easier and simpler when there is no resistance and a
soul is able to relax and accept what is going on, *knowing* that a process has
to take place—that there are no short cuts—that as each stage is reached it has
to be gone through before the final bringing forth of the New into the light
of day.

There has been a release of Cosmic Power which grows stronger every day.
This Cosmic Power, when it is recognised and accepted, brings great peace,
upliftment, illumination and revelation. When resisted it brings chaos and
confusion into the lives of individuals as well as into the world situation. Look
around you. All is complete turmoil. Every country is undergoing violent
changes—greed, jealousy, hatred, unrest of every kind are rampant everywhere.
Every emotion is growing in intensity.

It is vitally important to watch yourself with the greatest care. Watch your
reactions and see that they are loving and positive. Realise the work you are
doing as Lightbearers. Realise its importance. Each day, as you unite and
send forth the Light, a vital work is being done; as you do this consciously it
is even more effective. Never think that the time spent radiating Light is
wasted. You can do this work individually at all times, during the day and
during the night—not a second is wasted. Consciously send out Light and
more Light, Love and more Love. to individuals, to groups, to countries, to
the world. The need is great; therefore the need must be answered.

It does not matter what you are doing. You can become consciously aware of
an individual, of a country or whatever it may be and channel Light and Love
towards it. You may be peeling potatoes, digging in the garden or doing the
hundred and one things which need to be done, but you can still be used at
any time. Remember that you are on duty twenty-four hours a day, so be on
the alert and sensitive to the needs around you. You see a need—answer it!

91

Do all for My sake and be All. Reflect My Light and Love like beacons in a darkened world bringing hope and comfort to the many.

ACCORDING TO YOUR FAITH

1.   According to your faith be it unto you. What you know is true—is true. As a man thinketh so is he. When you accept this you are able to do all things and there is no limit to what can be manifested in My name.

You will find in the days ahead that many seeds of Light which have been sown in souls and are lying dormant in the darkness will now begin to germinate, emerging out of the darkness into glorious Light. Great changes will take place in many hearts, very unexpected changes. The hardest hearts will soften and once again Love will flow freely.

There will be a great uniting and linking together of the forces of Light. There will be a breaking up of many old groups but there will be a re-forming of new groups where the Light of Truth shall gather those of the Light together forming an unbreakable band of Lightbearers.

The old shall pass away and you shall behold the New in all its wonder and glory. You shall *know* that victory is at hand and is assured. Shout with joy and let your hearts sing with gratitude.

DO YOU BELIEVE?

2.   My Beloveds, do you believe with all your hearts, minds and souls that I AM in you and you are in Me, that we are One in Spirit and in Truth? Then you do indeed know the Truth and walk in the Truth.

Accept the Truth in complete childlike faith and it fills you with such abounding joy that you feel the limitlessness of My Love.

Take heed and watch yourself. Speak no idle words but only words of wisdom and truth. Silence is golden when filled with love for Me.

Waste no time in idle thinking or dreaming. Realise that within you you have all power, all intelligence, all wisdom, all understanding, that you draw from the very source of Universal Mind and Universal Consciousness.

Seek and you shall find and nothing shall be concealed from you. Be at peace.

BE STILL—TUNE IN—LISTEN

3.   Tune in to Me daily and hourly, minute by minute. See that there is no interference and that the contact is true. See that your 'set' is perfectly adjusted—miss nothing, for this contact is your lifeline. It is as vital to you as the breath of your body which is Life.

You can cut yourself off from Me as easily and quickly as you can switch off a radio set, but remember—you are the one who does it—never blame anyone else. When you are not in tune, look within yourself and see what has gone wrong. Do some adjusting and be in perfect attunement again. Be still, re-attune and listen. Gradually you will be able to pick up where you left off. As you do so, you will find a great peace and joy infil you as you are again in clear contact with your divine Source. It becomes more and more important to keep this close contact with Me. Give constant thanks for all that is happening and see My hand in everything.

DRAW NIGH UNTO ME AND I WILL DRAW NIGH UNTO THEE

4.   My Beloveds, draw nigh unto Me and I will draw nigh unto thee. Each time you become aware of Me you are drawing nigh unto Me, you are feeling and knowing the Source of your true being. You are aware of our Oneness, our Union, that there is no separation. We are One and that *you* are part of the Whole.

You are a branch of the Tree of Life and you live and move and have your being as part of the Tree. You are aware that if you were cut off from that Tree you would be as nothing and would wither and die, but as long as you realise that you are part of that Tree you function as one with it. You flower and flourish in full perfection, drawing your all from Me, the Source of all Life, all Being.

I say to each one of you: draw night to Me. Draw your strength from Me at all times. Rely on Me for all and lean not on your own understanding.

The sending out of My word at this time is vitally important—far more important than any of you realise. Send forth these messages of Truth on wings of Light and Love, for I have gone before to prepare the way and all will fall on fertile and prepared ground.

All is in My hands.

ENTER INTO THE SECRET PLACES OF THE MOST HIGH

5.   There is so much going on on the outer planes that these times of withdrawal are most important, these times of entering into the 'secret place of the Most High'. There in the peace and silence you can re-adjust your whole being, draw on the source of all power and return refreshed and revitalised, ready to cope with all that lies ahead of you.

Every soul needs these times of re-adjustment. Some realise this, others do not and busy themselves in great activities which exhaust them until they become like rundown clocks that need rewinding. Unless they go into the silence for rewinding they become ineffective and eventually stop ticking. The hours spent alone with Me are vital for the work being done for Me and are vital for your spiritual advancement. These times alone with Me are your meat and drink, they are the food of the Spirit which enables you to do what has to be done with courage and without hesitation.

Stand firm and be of good cheer, for in the days to come the storms will rage all around you but you will remain steadfast and unaffected by them because your faith and trust are firmly rooted and grounded in Me. The days ahead will be challenging and invigorating. See that your anchors have been cast out and have sunk deep so that they will hold fast no matter how wild the storms. I cannot have you breaking loose in the midst of the storms or you would be dashed upon the rocks. Those who put their full trust and faith in Me can weather the storms ahead. I need you prepared and in readiness. Be at peace.

You will find a great bond of unity and oneness growing up between all centres. Each has a specific part to play in the whole but all are united in the Light. Allow nothing to divide you. All must follow their inner guidance. You are part of a perfect whole. Expand your consciousness and you will see and appreciate what is happening. Do not become insular; this is a Universal operation and every Lightbearer is involved.

Think Victory. Live Victory. Be Victory and behold Victory.

Lightbearers of the Universe—UNITE.

HOW MANY TIMES HAVE I TOLD YOU?

6.　　My Beloveds—be very still and in that perfect stillness listen to what I have to say, take heed and obey My instructions. What is the use of being given instructions if you do not use them? Day by day I lead you into the paths of righteousness, I guide your feet into the ways of Light and Truth, I fill your hearts full of My divine Love—but action has to be taken and *you* have to put into practice and live what you know.

How many times have I told you that you cannot expect everything to fall into your lap without lifting a finger? You each have your part to play and only by playing it to the full can you expect wonders to come about. Put the wheels in motion, do your part and then you cna leave the rest to Me. I must have your full co-operation. I need hands and feet to work in and through. Sometimes you are inclined to forget this. My channels are vitally important.

Let My Love and Light and Wisdom abound. Praise be.

I AM THE VINE

7.　Always remember that I AM the Vine and you are the branches. I AM the Source of All. You can do all things through Me but without Me you are as nothing. With Me you are all things and can do all things. Never separate yourselves from Me in thought, word or deed. Seek that complete Oneness with Me and abide in it forever and ever.

Abide in Me and I in you and *know* that great shall be the works that you shall do in My Name. Miracle upon miracle shall come about. The Light shall shine forth for all to see and they shall be drawn to the Light and shall abide in the Light and there shall be no darkness.

The time has come when all shall recognise Me in all that is taking place. You do what has to be done because I ask you to do it. All My promises shall come about. I withhold nothing from those who believe and do My will.

LET YOUR EYE BE SINGLE

8.　Let your eye be single to My glory and your whole being shall be filled with Light. There shall be no darkness in you and your being, which is filled with Light, shall comprehend all things. Your understanding will expand day by day as your mind is stayed on Me.

As you seek, hidden secrets will be revealed and the power which has been lying dormant and which is within all men shall stir and awaken out of its slumbers. The gates of Heaven shall be swung wide open and My Heaven shall be brought down upon Earth.

The most glorious pattern is being woven at this time. You may not see its true perfection yet, but I AM the Master Weaver and I assure you that every thread is falling into place in the most wonderful way and the pattern is growing and evolving. When the Whole has been completed you will be astounded at the wonder of it.

Now is the time of the resurrection—Light, Light and more Light. Praise be.

LOVE BRINGS UNITY

9.　Wait upon Me at all times and in all places, for I AM with you always. As you seek Me, so will you find Me there in the very midst of you. Open your hearts and bring Peace, Joy and Love to all those you contact. See them with eyes of purest love. See the best in them and know them as My beloved children.

Judge no one—be critical of no one. Raise your consciousness until you can see the Allness of All, the Oneness of the One, Love your enemies, love your fellowmen, see them as One in My divine Love. The more Love that flows out into the world from each individual soul, the more help you are to your fellowmen.

Love brings unity, peace of heart and mind. Love heals all wounds.

With Love in your hearts and a complete surrendering of yourselves to Me, I can use you as channels to help many souls in darkness. When you sit in peace together each day you become a tremendous power. As the vibrations rise you open yourselves and allow Me to use you to channel My divine Love and Light out into the world and into the lives of individuals.

You feel the tremendous linking up of the forces of Light all over the world. You feel the links becoming stronger every day. You are My Lightbearers and wherever the Light is taken, the darkness is dispersed.

Let the Light of Truth be thrown on every situation, for darkness cannot withstand the Light. Never take one another for granted. When Love is flowing there is always appreciation—let that be expressed. A word of love and appreciation goes a long way.

Flexibility is necessary. Unite and be positive. Let your lives be a song of praise, joy, glory and thanksgiving.

LOVE IS THE KEY

10.   Get into harmony with Universal Life. Blend into the perfection of Life eternal. You are from everlasting to everlasting—accept this truth, sink into it, absorb it into your being and become one with it. Accept it with the Spirit—live and move and have your being in the Spirit. Raise your consciousness at all times until you feel yourselves completely at one with your fellowmen. Know that there is no separation, that you are all One in Me. Feel My divine Love flowing through you, welding you, uniting you into One Being.

Each day surrender yourselves anew to Me, to My service. Lay your whole being before Me and offer yourselves to Me to use as I will. A re-dedication is necessary; then everything becomes alive and vital and nothing is taken for granted. You know that when you are taken for granted or take anything for granted, life becomes stale, dull and lifeless, but when you appreciate everything and are appreciated, everything changes and glows and becomes Light— life becomes worth living and is good. So why not now, in this very moment of time, surrender your whole life and living to Me anew? There is no time like the present in which to take action.

Having done that, go your way rejoicing with a new sense of freedom—with joy in your heart ready to do anything I ask of you. Accept this as a new day and dwell not on the past—there is far too much to be done in the ever present Now, the glorious Now. See My hand in everything that is taking place and say; "Thank You." You can never say "Thank You" too often!

Open your hearts wide and let them be ever loving, ever grateful hearts for everything that is happening. When you do this all difficulties are overcome, all obstacles are surmounted. Nothing can stand in the way of an open, loving and grateful heart.

Love is the key that opens all doors. *You* have the key. Use it all the time until all doors have been unlocked and know that no door can remain closed when the 'Key of Love' is placed in the lock and firmly turned.

Do what has to be done with My authority and be not fearful, for I AM with you always. Know that all things are possible. Miss nothing. Do what has to be done wholeheartedly. When I AM put first in everything, all else falls into place perfectly. Be at peace.

LOVE ME AND DO MY WILL

11.   Seek deep within a soul and there you will see clearly the need of that soul. Then let My divine Love pour through you to heal the hurts and wounds until all is Light and Peace in the heart of that soul. Judge no man by his outer appearance but seek deep within to find the true Self.

Many will come seeking and some will not know what it is they seek. Therefore there must be awareness and sensitivity in *you*. You will know what your part is, so step forward and when you have done what is required step quietly back and let someone else play his part.

Stop and look at those around you and let your heart be filled with gratitude. When all are united in their highest beliefs (no matter what their beliefs, creed, sects or colour), you see the true Brotherhood of Man because you know that I AM the true Fatherhood of Man—all are One in Me and there is no separation.

I need you free, free, free. I cannot use you unless you are free—please remember this.

Love Me and do My will.

MAKE ROOM FOR THE NEW

12.   Blessed are they who hear My Word and follow it, for from this every action springs. What is the use of hearing My Word, reading it, pondering

upon it unless you live it in your daily lives, bringing Me into everything you do, sharing all with Me?

Is there anything you would be ashamed to lay before Me? If there is, in deep humility bring it forth into the Light of Truth and let it be transmuted.

Cast the old away—make room for the New. Open your eyes and behold Nature all around you. A tree has to rid itself of all dead leaves before new growth can spring into full glory. The seed must break through its old skin before it can grow and flourish. When a chick hatches out of its shell, it does not cling to the shell but leaves it behind forever, and is transformed into a new life.

So it is with each one of you—leave the old behind as you advance into the New.

There are times when I tell you to be flexible and to have no fixed ideas, to make room for something entirely different and new. This is important. Keep open, ready to accept change without reluctance. Accept the fact that there is a right time for everything and leave it in My hands.

Take nothing for granted. Lift up your hearts and know I AM with you always. Be about My business, doing My will and walking in My ways.

MY WAYS ARE THE WAYS OF SPIRIT

13.   All that you do, do for My sake. Let your loyalties be undivided. Let your eye be single so that your whole being is filled with Light—My Light, My Truth, My Love. This is the only way to live. This is your destiny.

Find freedom in doing My will and you will find yourself bursting forth like a perfect flower, growing in stature and in wholeness. There are many different aspects of My work but until you are ready I wait in infinite patience. The choice lies in your hands. You each have free will. I simply have to wait.

Raise your consciousness, expand your thinking, open your hearts and let nothing stand in the way. My ways are the ways of the Spirit.

I know what is best for each one of you. Therefore give all and receive all.

TAKE TIME

14.   Take time to be alone with Me, to be still, to feel Me, to know Me and to love Me. Take time to enjoy life to the full, to count your blessings and to give thanks for them. Take time to know one another and love one another as I love you.

You do not pay to see the beauties of a glorious sunrise or sunset. You do not pay to see Nature springing up and bursting into bud at this time. But stop and take time to open your eyes—look and see—and glory in what you see. The beauties are there all around you to gladden your soul, lift your thinking, to bring joy and light into your living.

Take time to do these things, to seek deep within and find Me. See My hand in everything that is happening. See My promises and My truths being manifested all around you and give thanks. Know that I am working in many hearts. Time is as nothing in My sight and yet unless I remind you to take time to do these things you will let life rush past and miss so much. I want you to enjoy *everything* to the full. Take time to dwell on these words and live them forever.

THE FIRST AND GREATEST COMMANDMENT

15.   My beloveds, the first and greatest commandment is to love Me, the Lord your God, with all your heart, with all your soul and with all your mind. The second is to love your neighbour as yourself. There are no commandments greater than these. When you fulfil these commandments all other things follow naturally. The first proves our Oneness and the second tells you to recognise it in all mankind.

Always remember that simplicity is the essence of perfection. The more you love Me, the more you love your fellow man. The more you love, the greater the joy you find in life, until life is filled with joy and happiness. When you love and pour it forth in great abundance, so it will be returned to you. Everyone responds to a loving joyous heart. When Love is flowing, life is full to overflowing—so love, love, love.

THE PILGRIM

16.   The greatest thing you can do for any soul is to turn him within and enable him to find his true Self, to enable him to find Me within the depths of his being. Let each soul seek within and there find the solution to every problem, the answer to every query.

It helps no one to be spoonfed all the time. The time comes when each one must stand on his own feet, know within himself exactly where he is going and what his goal in life is. You can take a soul so far along the spiritual path and then leave that soul to walk by himself, learn by himself, to seek for understanding, knowledge, deep within. He may stumble and fall many times but he must learn to pick himself up, dust himself off and stride forward with renewed strength and determination.

A pilgrim along the spiritual path must never faint or fail along the way, never look back and hanker for the old ways, imagining they were easier. Cast off the old cloak and put on a new shining one, one that will light every step of the way.

TO KNOW IS TO MANIFEST

17.   A simple faith, a simple *knowing* is all that is needed to bring forth My truths and manifest them in your lives and in your living. Change your thinking and you will see how simple life can be. Let the I AM become a reality to you, a part of you, so that there is no separateness and all is Oneness.

Absorb these truths, until at last you identify yourselves completely with Me and know your divine heritage, that I AM within you, that I AM yours and you are Mine forever. Much orthodox teaching has to be thrown out of your lives. Things which you were taught at your mother's knee you now have to see in a completely new light. It is more difficult for the orthodox Christian to move into the New than for one who has no belief. Old beliefs become ingrained but they have to go as you move into the New.

Be not impatient with yourselves when you find yourselves still with old conceptions clinging to you. Never leave a vacuum; replace the old with something new instantly. See the goal before you and know that you *will* reach it come what may.

This is the art of living, the art of manifestation. *Know* and never allow doubt to enter. To *know* is to manifest. When you *know,* you have seen on the inner what is to be brought down on to the outer and *it is so.*

See the best and manifest it. Be at peace and in the stillness let Me reveal Myself in and through you.

TORCHBEARERS

18.   You are like torchbearers who have lit their torches from the Eternal Flame. Nothing and no one can extinguish those torches held on high for Me. The rain may fall, the hail may batter, the wind may blow, but those torches once alight cannot be extinguished, for they are lit by My Cosmic Flame which is forever and forever.

You will see these fortresses of Light all over the world coming into their own. You will realise why there has had to be this long process of preparation in establishing these Light Centres so that they would be in readiness for these days ahead. The radiations which have been put into them have deep and unshakable foundations.

These places of Light will be fully protected. Be ready. These places will draw many souls to them and they will come from far and wide. The doors must not be closed to them. They come not only for refuge but to give as well. Each one will have something to contribute and they must be allowed to play their part no matter how small or mundane it may appear to be.

Remember what I have told you—Light will attract Light—so you will know that those who are drawn to them are of the Light. Judge no one.

"By their fruits ye shall know them" and the children of Light shall be gathered together and great shall be their rejoicing, for all shall do My will and walk in My ways, finding peace and joy in their hearts and minds.

Peace, be still and KNOW ME.

WITHOUT VISION

19. Without vision the people perish. It is vital for you to have vision, that you see things clearly and bring them about. Idle thoughts get you nowhere. Raise your consciousness and let your vision be of higher things, things of the Spirit, for as you sow so shall you reap. Sow seeds of Love and Joy and reap those fruits.

Take time to look for the best and count your blessings. Raise your eyes to the heavens and see Me in the stars, in the sun and in the moon. See Me in the grain of sand, in the soil, in the leaf and in the flower. Look and you will see Me in everything and your whole being will be filled with joy and thanksgiving. Open your eyes and see. Open your ears and hear. It is there for all to enjoy when they choose to do so.

GOD SPOKE TO ME
Part Four

INTRODUCTION

My Beloveds, as life becomes more intensified, more alive, more vital, you must enjoy it to the full. All this is happening now and these feelings become stronger every day. No wonder you feel these tremendous changes taking place within you and all around you! Your physical bodies are also undergoing changes which result in a certain amount of discomfort, so do not be concerned about this.

Many souls are going through changes at this time, making them highly sensitive and more alert to all that goes on. These changes may make you emotional, causing you to feel things deeply and strongly but do not let this worry you. You will soon be over the 'highs and lows' and will find yourselves on a more even keel and so you will be able to help others who are going through similar experiences. You will have a deeper understanding and perceptiveness and will see where help is needed almost before the soul in need has realised it himself. Keep your feelers out and waving around you so that you can be of help to your fellowmen on this similar path.

Outwardly you can see the tremendous progress that is being made but I want you to realise that this outer progress would mean nothing without all that is going on within the Inner. What is now being manifested on the outer has already manifested in true perfection on the inner planes.

As above, so below—what is being done now is simply bringing down My Heaven upon Earth step by step.

One day in the future you will be able to do this by the power of thought without all the physical work involved. When you fully understand the power of thought and learn to use it in the right way, these powers will be yours to use for My work and to My honour and glory. All these powers are to be used for the benefit of mankind. Mankind has to learn to use them aright and never for the self or for self-glorification. Never imagine that this is impossible because I tell you that nothing is impossible and that these powers will be yours to use for My work in the days to come.

Remember always that you are moving further and further into the new. Never limit anything; expand your consciousness until you see and feel these things taking place now. As you think, so you are and so you create in form. Nothing can stand in the way of My creation.

Let My peace and My Love infil and enfold each one of you. Let your lives be a song of praise, joy, glory and thanksgiving. Be at peace and see the best in everyone and in everything.

Draw it forth—Love—Love—Love.

AS A MAN THINKETH

1.   Always remember that as a man thinketh, so he will become. You hold within you all power and when you are ready to use it rightly it is all yours. The seeds you sow will spring forth; so see that those seeds are positive loving ones, that they are pure, good and unadulterated.

As you think, so do you create; this is My law. This is a principle which needs to be understood and put into practice in everyday living.

Remember that it is not enough to take a handful of seeds and scatter them on the gournd. When you want a good crop you take time to prepare the ground, to dig and nourish it before the planting takes place. So it is with the soul; it needs to be prepared before the seeds of the Spirit are planted in it.

Many souls think that if they go to church once a week, say their prayers at night and spend a few minutes in quiet with Me, that is enough to carry them through this life. That is like raking over the top of the ground, planting seeds in unprepared ground and hoping they will grow. So it is with a soul whose heart and mind are not stayed on Me, whose faith is not strong, who allows doubt and fears to come in. When the time for testing comes, that soul will be unable to withstand. Therefore be grateful for the training you have been given.

A CIRCLE

2.   As it was in the beginning, is now and ever shall be, life is eternal with no beginning and no end. You just begin to grasp the wonder of this truth. A circle has no beginning and no end but goes on and on. So it is with life; as you were in the beginning so you are now. You have gone the full cycle. You have now become aware of your divinity which lies within every soul but which has lain dormant for too long.

In the beginning there was no separation and all was one. We walked and talked together in perfect unity and harmony. You knew you were a part of Me and functioned in that complete oneness. It has meant breaking the bonds of old conceptions and teachings, of raising your consciousness so that the old is left behind and you enter into another dimension where all is one, where there is no duality, where you can say and mean, with every atom of your being, "God I AM" and there is nothing else. This truth is there for all to claim.

Fear nothing. Expand and accept this truth as *your* truth and as *your* true heritage. In true humility, stand before Me and recognise Me. By- accepting this truth you are freeing yourself of all that has bound you down the ages. You enter into the great light, becoming part of that great light, functioning in it and from it. The spark is no longer separate but part of the Divine Whole.

Be at peace. Know that this is what is happening now and live fully in the now. Open your hearts, claim these wonderful truths, become one with Me and rejoice.

A STATE OF SERENITY

3.   Seek deep within and find that peace which passeth understanding. Remain in that state of consciousness so that nothing outward can touch or ruffle your serenity, for it is when you are in this state that I can work in and through you. You cannot see yourself reflected within a turbulent pool but when that water has been stilled and becomes like a mirror, you can see the reflection of yourself perfectly. Still your soul until you reflect nothing but the perfect, My Love, My Light, My Wisdom. In this state of consciousness, you can be used to radiate those attributes to your fellowmen.

You have started on this path. Know that practice makes perfect; be patient, be persistent, persevere. Without constant practice you cannot hope to achieve. No pianist, singer or artist ever reached the pinnacle of perfection without hours of practice, without repetition.

It would be useless to remain wrapped in cotton wool all your life. You need a loving and understanding heart and this you find by weathering the rough with the smooth, by experiencing life at its heights and in its depths. Unless you have experienced, how can you hope to understand deeply? No lessons need be abortive; all have a place in the overall pattern and plan.

Step by step, tread this path with love in your hearts and perfection as your aim. Know that you will achieve and rejoice in that knowing.

BELIEVEST THOU?

4.   Believest thou that I have many truths to reveal to you? As you believe, so will it come about. I am guiding your feet into new paths and you begin to understand. things which you have heard and read many times but have not really understood. It was as if you were hard of hearing and had scales before your eyes and were unable to see or comprehend the true meaning of what was being presented to you. Now, like a new born kitten, you are slowly

opening your eyes to the world of truth. What you see are the things of the Spirit and you slowly begin to understand and grasp these things of the Spirit as they become a part of you.

The immensity of the worlds which are being lit for you from within are bringing great light to your understanding. Things which have had little meaning in the past are becoming illumined by the Light of Truth and many things will fall into place in the days to come. You begin to know and to demonstrate in your daily living the power of manifestation.

Keep raising your consciousness, stretching and growing spiritually. Ignore the growing pains; keep your thoughts positive and loving.

The sorting and sifting takes place now at great speed. Realise that time is short and there is no time to be wasted. Be not disappointed if some reject My Word. Life becomes more confusing outwardly; therefore the only place in which to find the answer is deep within. The greater the outer confusion, the more still you must become so that the words, "Be still and know Me" become alive within you.

Take heed of My words and live them twenty-four hours a day.

BE STILL AND LISTEN

5.   Be still and listen. I ask for nothing more. When you become still, you become emptied of all, emptied of the old and ready to be refilled with the new. As long as you are straining and striving you are not free or empty and there is no room for the new to enter. You cannot put new wine into old bottles, you cannot put an old piece of cloth on a new garment, any more than you can be filled with the new while still clinging to the old! Become an empty vessel waiting to be filled with My Love, My Light and My Wisdom.

Do this at the beginning of each day. The moment you awaken, let the words: "Thy Will Be Done" be on your lips and in your heart. As you learn to do this a great peace will infil you. When your love for Me is paramount, your desire to do My Will will stop at nothing. You will do all I ask you to do and be all that I ask you to be. Then you are My instruments, My channels, and I can work in and through you.

Never limit Me in any way. I AM limitless. I AM all in all. Reflect Me. Become like a clear still pool. Reflect Me like a mirror.

Still your heart and mind. Still your whole being. Again I say to you, "Wait upon Me." It matters not how long you have to wait; wait until you hear My still small voice. You *can* hear it when you become still.

I AM ever with you. Become consciously aware of Me at all times. We are at one, one in heart, mind and spirit. You are consciously aware of the Divine Presence, the Christ within.

Be at peace. All this is taking place within you now. Great things are coming to pass within and without. My Kingdom is being brought down upon this Earth. You will indeed behold the new Heaven and the new Earth and great will be the rejoicing. All this is coming to pass at great speed now.

Open your eyes and behold My wonders. I tell you that these are tremendous days.

COMMUNICATION

6.   To love one another you must try to understand one another. To understand you must be able to communicate, whether that communication be through words or in silent action matters not, as long as it is done in love. You must be loving and tolerant towards your fellowmen.

When something is clear as crystal to you it does not mean that it is so to all. Therefore lovingly, with patience and understanding, try to convey what you are experiencing and share those deep feelings within you. It may not be easy to do this but make the effort. When you love you *want* to share with those you love.

Love is the answer to all relationships; without Love there cannot be communication. Where there is Love no words need be spoken. Where there is Love there are no language barriers. Love can be conveyed in action, a silent look, the smallest deed. Love is so great that it can be felt and sensed. When you truly love, you love all.

Many souls go through life and never know the meaning of Love. How blessed you are who know Love and who are loved! Love is the key that opens all doors, breaks down all barriers. Is it any wonder that I keep telling you to open your hearts and love one another? Compassion towards your fellowmen is not enough; there must be Love. Where there is Love, there am I, for I AM Love.

Know the meaning of Divine Love, and perfect understanding fills your whole being.

COSMIC POWER

7.   This is an exacting time for each of you, a time of deep changes within and without, a time of seeking and sorting, of moving into new realms and

new dimensions. This period of transition is not easy. You can help by accepting change without resistance. A flower does not resist when the bud splits and the bloom unfolds. What is waiting to unfold with each one is far more wonderful, more beautiful than any flower—and all is happening now.

This tremendous release of Cosmic Power has awakened within each one something which has been lying dormant and now has begun to germinate. Some are more aware than others. Some seeds take longer to germinate than others, but all do so in the end unless the life force has gone out of them. Therefore expect dramatic changes in individuals within and without.

You will see the seemingly impossible become possible, black turned to purest white, evil intent changed in mid-stream, man at last beginning to see the error of his ways. You will see him realise what he has done to affect the balance of Nature and he will want to rectify what he has done wrong. He will become awakened at last to the things that really matter in life, the things of the Spirit. Know that every change is for the best for all concerned.

FULFIL THIS LAW

8.   Remember that Love fulfils the Law. Fulfil this Law of Love and all others are fulfilled with it. Love is the greatest uniting power in the Universe. Love opens all doors. Love brings harmony and understanding where there is nothing but disharmony and misunderstanding. Open your hearts and let My divine Love flow freely. Express that divine Love in a hundred and one ways.

Realise that I AM in you, that nothing can separate us. We are One. Share everything with Me, your greatest joys, your greatest sorrows and your seeming failures. I ask for all, and when all is given, you will find the true freedom of the Spirit because there is absolutely nothing between us. Love flows freely and joy overflows where there is freedom. Pull down every barrier as quickly as possible so that nothing stands between thee and Me. Know the wonder of our Oneness.

Be not downcast because you feel that you have so far to go. Be thankful that you are ever moving, ever longing to attain truth. Know that because of that longing you cannot fail, you *will* get there in the end. You are not chasing the end of a rainbow; you are reaching for a goal and you *will* get there. Let the Light of truth shine, dispersing all darkness. Banish negative thoughts; they have no place in your life or in your living.

There is great turmoil in the world and there is greater to come. Realise that you are fully protected. Let My peace and love enfold each one of you. Let your lives be a song of praise, joy, glory and thanksgiving. Take heed of all I say. Live My Word and find peace and security in Me.

LOVING IS . . .

9.   Loving is living and living is loving. You cannot say that you love Me and not love your fellowmen. As you love your fellowmen, so do you love Me, for all are one. Accept this Oneness at all times. It gives great peace of heart and of mind when there is no division.

Accept victory at all times and defeat will vanish into nothingness. Expansion means people and this means caring for and loving them, seeing their needs and answering them. It means an expansion of heart power. Open your hearts and keep them open, allowing nothing to close them. The more you love Me, the more you will love those whom you contact and the more you will want to help them.

Look for the divine spark in every soul. It may not always be easy to find but know that it is there, and as you seek it so you will find it. Get into harmony with those around you; Love brings harmony, so love, love, love' The more Love there is flowing between you all, the greater will the peace and harmony be sensed and felt by those around you, those who come to you.

If at any time you are feeling out of harmony with the whole, remember that change can come in the twinkling of an eye. Change your attitude, change your thinking, and black will instantly turn to white. When a bright light is taken into a dark room the darkness disappears in the ray of the light and is no more.

The floodgates are wide open and My blessings are being poured upon you all the time.

MANY WAYS

10.   There are so many ways to the same goal. Find your way and follow it step by step, but be not critical of another's way. All of you are individuals; all of you should be doing your own thinking. All of you should be seeking deep within and finding the answer for you, not for anyone else. If you are doing this all the time, you will have no time to waste and when you eventually meet together at the goal there will be a rejoicing and a greater love and understanding flowing between you.

Let one thing follow the next with a sense of peace and rightness, so that stress and strain disappear into nothingness. Life should be effortless because it is guided and directed by Me.

It is a good exercise to try to express in words the deep experiences you are going through at this time. Do not hesitate to do this. Unless you try, you will not accomplish anything. What does it matter if no one understands what it is you are trying to share? Do it for My sake and for love of Me.

Those who are aware of this release of Cosmic Power are bound to find tremendous changes in their lives and living, in their thinking and understanding. Love and understanding are needed, so love and let it flow forth unceasingly.

MY HALLMARK

11.   All must have My hallmark of Love at this time. Many will come, many will prophesy, many will be the words written and spoken. There will be much conflict and confusion. Many contradictions and predictions will come to your attention and unless you are very aware and have your eyes wide open and your feelers out and know inwardly what is truth and what is false, you will be as the majority of mankind, swayed by every wind, lost, confused and confounded.

Be very still. Read and listen to all that comes to your notice. Never jump to conclusions. Never judge or condemn until you know from within what is the truth. The truth will always have My hallmark of Love imprinted on it and within it. Seek deep within you and you will be left in no doubt.

Again I say to you, "Seek My hallmark of Love in all things and you cannot be led astray." Unless those who speak or write in My Name do so in purest Love, they pronounce not the Truth. I tell you that things will not be plain sailing at this time unless each one seeks diligently and goes deep within. Many false trails will be laid but there will always be the right clues along the way; that is My Way—when the clues are sought. Seek for the signs of the Spirit and you cannot be misled.

NOW ARE YE THE SONS OF GOD

12.   Now are ye the sons of God. Now do you walk and talk with Me. Now do you listen to My voice. Do not wait for things to happen tomorrow or next year. They are happening to you now. When you live in the ever present now, you are building for the future without wasting time or taking thought of it, but by simply living it, living it, living it.

You know many truths in theory; now put them into practice and live them all the time. Man expects everything to go smoothly for him, expects to receive and take everything to the self without giving anything, but no soul is really living when he is getting all the time without giving in return.

Remember that each soul has something specific to give on different levels, so judge not any man on the outer. In fact, judge not at all! The ways of Spirit are contrary to man's ways. Seek ye the way of Spirit and be at peace.

ON WAKING EACH MORNING

13.   On waking each morning raise your whole being to Me, reach up in thought to the highest. Know that this day is blest by Me and as you take each step in it, become filled with My Light and walk in truth and understanding. Let your thoughts dwell only on the positive. Know that it will be a day fully blest by Me—and it will be.

In those waking moments you can set the pattern for the day. Do you lie there giving thanks for My good gifts, for all the blessings I pour down upon you, or do you bemoan the fact that it is just another day? How you react to those first moments can colour your whole day with beauty, wonder, glory, all that is perfect and positive, or with negativity. Watch yourself carefully each morning as you awaken and bring down upon you all the best of your summit thinking. Carry this throughout the day, filling it with the best.

As you close your eyes at night never forget to give thanks for all that has happened during the day. Bring out the highlights of the day and dwell on them with gratitude. See how they have affected your life and those of others. Take with you into your sleep state a grateful, loving and understanding heart. Raise your consciousness and let your thoughts dwell upon Me, and then you can only think the best.

When you are faced with what appears to be an insurmountable problem, raise your consciousness and view the problem from that raised state. Then you will see it in a different light and will see how to surmount it. Realise that there is always a way out and never give up until you have found it.

Be still and let Me use you as I will. Let My will be done.

PRESERVE YOUR SENSE OF HUMOUR

14.   Life is a constant giving and receiving, a constant inhaling and exhaling of the breath of life. You could not spend your entire time inhaling without

exhaling any more than you could spend your time giving without receiving. When life ceases to be a two-way thing it dries up and dies away. Every soul has to learn to live a life, and group living brings this out very clearly. No soul can live entirely for himself; he has to learn to live for others and with others. There must be a constant giving and receiving on all levels in order for perfect peace and harmony to be maintained.

Each one gives on a different level and in a different way, so there must be no comparing or criticising of one another. As each one is guided from within, he will know what his part is within the whole and will quietly and silently go ahead to do what has to be done. There must be a constant seeking within and a great sensitivity and awareness developed in order to enable this to come about. There must be balance in all things and at all times.

Never let life become too serious or too earnest. See the lighter side and have a sense of humour. I tell you that there must be laughter and joy in living. Let joy abound. When you feel joy bubbling in you, let it come out and share it with those around you. Joy is contagious! One soul bubbling with joy can affect everyone else so let it bubble over!

Never suppress your feelings of true happiness and thankfulness; express them in words and actions and let there be more joy. There is always a light and funny side to everything if you look for it.

When you learn to live fully in the moment without thought of tomorrow, your life will indeed be filled with love, joy and harmony.

Bubble up and bubble over and enjoy life to the full.

REVIEW YOUR RELATIONSHIPS WITH THOSE AROUND YOU

15.   Realise that you cannot help a soul unless that soul really wants help and is ready to be helped. I tell you to send that soul nothing but Love and more Love. Be still and wait, but be there when that soul turns for help.

When you are training a small child to do up his shoes, for example, you have to be patient and watch him fumbling about with the laces. You have to sit and watch, encouraging him from time to time, showing him how it can be done without actually doing it for him, until finally, in triumph, he masters the art!

Great patience is needed, not only with the one who is learning but by the one who is doing the teaching as well. If you do everything for a child he will never learn, never stand on his own feet and be independent, but will rely on you to do everything for him.

So it is with a soul on the spiritual path. I have to sit back patiently and watch each soul make one mistake after another without interfering in any way, but when that soul cries out for help, I am there in an instant to encourage, to comfort and direct but never doing everything for that soul. All must learn to do their own work, but with Me to guide and to direct. Be not dismayed or disheartened when you see a soul take the wrong path. Realise that it has some important lessons to learn and will learn more quickly in that way than in any other.

Getting cross, impatient and irritable helps no one. There is much to learn. You never stop learning all through life. Allow nothing to defeat you. Be determined to win through to victory and you will do so.

From time to time, review your relationships with those around you. Review your motives and your attitudes. Look within before blaming anyone else. See what you can do personally to right a wrong, and do it instantly. Don't wait for the other person to make the first move. Have a good spring cleaning every now and again and start afresh.

As you think, so you are. Think loving, positive thoughts and see the sunshine break through and permeate everything with light, dispelling the dark clouds and bringing beauty and harmony everywhere.

It is so easy to say, "Love one another" but it is a different matter really to do this.

BE AT PEACE AND CREATE PEACE ALL AROUND YOU.
SEEK UNITY

16.   Seek unity at all times, for where there is unity there is strength. Deep spiritual strength is needed to do what has to be done at this time. There can be no division, no wavering, but an absolute certainty deep within that what you are doing is right and guided by Me. With that certainty you can stride forward without hesitation and do what has to be done.

I am guiding all that you do at this time. There is nothing haphazard in what is happening. There is a clear pattern and plan running through everything. Do what has to be done because you know that united you stand.

These are critical times for all concerned. The world situation is critical, this country's situation is critical and this group situation also. I tell you yet again that there must be complete harmony and unity within the group so that those outside can batter hard but will find no weak links through which to cause havoc.

115

This release of Cosmic Power is bound to affect souls in many ways, bringing out the best in some and the worst in others, depending on the way they respond. My ways are strange, but remember that they are wonderful. Walk in them with a sure and firm tread. I AM with you always.

THE "NEVERS"

17. Never waste time seeking for the answer to life without. Seek within. There you will find Me in the midst of you and there you will find the answer to every question and every problem. There is no need to be bewildered when you turn within for the answer; when you learn to do this it will not matter whether you are alone on a desert island or in the middle of a crowded city, you will have the answer. Within you, you have a world no one can disturb. Secretly, silently you can withdraw into that world where you are completely One with Me and there find perfect peace and understanding.

When you have established yourself there, you can go into the world and be of real help to those whom you contact. You are taking with you that peace that passeth understanding; you are reflecting My Love and Light and Wisdom; you are bringing the Light of Truth to those who sit in darkness.

I withhold nothing from him who earnestly desires to find the truth. I cannot impress this upon you strongly enough. When you truly understand and accept this, you hold the answer to all there is within you. You understand the limitlessness of My Love, of My supply of all things. You see the best and manifest the best. Never place a limit or restriction on anything. You find your consciousness expanding, seeing everything that is beautiful, everything that is perfect, and by so doing you draw it to you.

This is the art of manifestation. You will learn to do this more and more in the days to come and so bring about My law of limitless supply. Raise your thinking, expand your consciousness, know the source of your supply, and your whole attitude will change in the twinkling of an eye. Remember this in the days ahead and let your faith and trust be rocklike and unshakable.

Never contemplate limitations or restrictions. Visualise the expansion coming first in one direction and then in another. You are manifesting My Heaven upon this Earth.

THE TRUTH SHALL SET YOU FREE

18. The truth shall set you free. You ask where you can find that truth? I tell you—deep within. Where can you find wisdom and understanding? Again

I say—within. When you are ready to receive the truth it is there waiting for you. Expand your consciousness and accept it.

You do not have to pay a price for these qualities. They are all yours, they always have been and always shall be, but they lie dormant until you claim them as your own.

When you claim them, a light shines forth from you into this darkened world. A light which has been burning low becomes brighter for all to see until you become as a beacon of Light, drawing other lights to you, forming an ever-increasing Light-band wherever you go. Light attracts Light, and darkness disappears into nothingness where there is Light. Reflect My Light, My Love and My Understanding and be a real help to your fellowmen who are groping their way in darkness. When the Light of Truth is shed on a situation, all fears and frustrations disappear.

You are here in this world to help, not hinder, your fellowmen. Cease all criticism, all judgment, all intolerance, and see only the perfect in each one. See the God-spark within each one and fan it until it grows into a flame.

Care must be taken in the handling of Light, whereas Love can go anywhere and everywhere. Love can tread where angels fear. Souls respond to Love even though they may try to hide the fact with a facade. Love and Light must work in close co-operation, for one needs the other. Balance is essential in order to bring results.

Watch My perfect plan unfold. I withhold nothing from those who love Me.

WAIT UPON ME AND FIND PEACE OF HEART AND MIND

19.   Feel My divine Light grow stronger and stronger within you and My divine Love flow in ever increasing power and force within you, through you and out into a world in desperate need. Keep yourselves open at all times so that you can be used in this way. Close not the doors of your hearts at any time; see that they remain wide open, for I can only work in open hearts. There is much work to be done in this torn and bleeding world. I have to work through channels and you are My channels. Never forget this.

Be ever grateful for every deep inner experience which raises your conscious-ness and makes you more aware of Me deep within you. Seek not for Truth without, but seek it within. In stillness you will find it. Take time to be still.

Never say that you are a seeker after truth and then fail to be still and seek in the right place. When the desire is great enough, you will allow nothing to stand in the way of your search for Truth. You will cease talking about it, cease discussing it; quietly you will go away alone and will take time to be still and seek within.

There must always be the perfect balance between the inner work and the outer. Never neglect either. See that they dovetail perfectly one with the other. You have the balance of sleeping and waking, of activity and of inactivity. Otherwise you would become unbalanced and this can happen if you are not watchful.

In group living this perfect balance is essential. Only in this way can things go smoothly, so take time to be still no matter how busy you are. Take time to be alone and seek Me and know Me.

Every now and again I have to remind you that you are pioneering the New Age in group living, that what you are working out now will be used by many. You will make mistakes, but you will learn from them and so help others. Time is getting short and there is no time to be wasted by making the same mistakes twice.

There are many changes taking place in all of you. Love one another as I love you. Work together for the good of the whole with never a thought of the self. Group living is selfless living. joyous living, light living.

My ways are perfect. Walk in them and rejoice, rejoice, rejoice.

WORK ON EVERY LEVEL

20.　The work being done at this time is of vital importance and greater than any of you imagine. All must be done in purest Love. When I speak of work, I speak of it on every level. Let there be joy in all you do.

A tremendous linking up is now taking place of Light bearers all over the world. Never has there been such a linking up. It is as if all the forces of Light are being drawn together to form an invincible Band of Light to withstand the oncoming rush of darkness. The greater the Light, the stronger the linking up and the greater the defeat. Where there is Light no darkness can enter, for darkness fades into nothingness when Light is present. Let Light move out to the four corners of the Earth completely encircling it.

See victory as the ultimate aim and know that the forces of Light will win *no* matter how hard the going may be at times. "Light Bearers of the World Unite." Let that be your cry. Hold high the Banner of Light for all to follow.

A great work is being done and even greater work will be done. All the training and the preparation which each one of you has undergone throughout the ages will now be drawn forth and used to the full. You will realise how vitally important all that severe training has been and lift up your heart in thankfulness.

All must be strong, unshakable and immovable to withstand what has to come. You will be tested to the hilt. All will go through the fiery furnace till the dross is burnt away and only the gold remains. Hallelujah!

YOUR BODIES ARE MY HOLY TEMPLE

21. Your bodies are My Holy Temple. Therefore they must be treated with love and respect, for this is holy ground and I AM within My Temple. Raise your consciousness until you can see this truth clearly. That which is within My Holy Temple is perfect, is in complete unity, harmony and oneness with the All in All. The more you concentrate your thoughts on these facts, the sooner you will see the reality of this truth. You understand many of these truths in theory, but theory is not enough. You must know them in practice and bring them into your daily living.

Little by little, My wondrous truths are becoming a part of you, and you begin to live and have your being in them. For many years I have repeated the same things in different words and you have wondered why. Now you begin to understand, for only by repetition has it become a part of you and is now becoming a reality to you.

As you sit in stillness, much can be revealed to you. That is why stillness is so vital, why it is so necessary to spend time alone with Me. This is life—life eternal to *you*. You have reached the point in your lives when it is as essential to you as breathing. Never hesitate to slip away and be still on your own.

Every soul needs these times of being completely alone with Me. You will find that the majority of people do not like being alone. They prefer to be with others, to be amongst noise, to be busy. They are afraid to be alone. They may make the excuse that they like being sociable, that they like being with people, but were you to see deep into their hearts, you would find their fear of being alone for any length of time. This is the state that man has got himself into. He does not find it easy to be alone in complete silence. His greatest need is simply to be still, to know Me and to take time with Me.

Often you hear it said that there are not hours enough in the day to do all that has to be done. This is not true. Stop and consider what you really do with those hours. See where you are wasting precious time in doing unguided things. When every moment of your time is guided by Me, everything gets done perfectly. Feelings of pressure are released and peace descends upon you. I AM WITH YOU ALWAYS.